P9-EIE-404

AMERICAN OAK FURNITURE

STYLES AND PRICES

BOOK II

SECOND EDITION

ROBERT W. AND
HARRIETT SWEDBERG

Other books by Robert W. and Harriett Swedberg

American Clocks and Clockmakers
American Oak Furniture Styles and Prices, revised edition
American Oak Furniture Styles and Prices, Book III
Antiquing in England: A Guide to Antique Centres
Collectors Encyclopedia of American Furniture, Volume I
Country Furniture and Accessories with Prices
Country Furniture and Accessories with Prices, Book II
Country Pine Furniture Styles and Prices, revised edition
Country Store 'N' More
Furniture of the Depression Era
Off Your Rocker
Tins 'N' Bins
Victorian Furniture Styles and Prices, revised edition
Victorian Furniture Styles and Prices, Book II
Victorian Furniture Styles and Prices, Book III
Wicker Furniture Styles and Prices, revised edition

Copyright © 1991, 1984 by Robert W. and Harriett Swedberg
Second edition   All Rights Reserved
Published in Radnor, Pennsylvania 19089, by Wallace-Homestead,
a division of Chilton Book Company

Photographs by the authors; printing and enlarging by Tom Luse
Manufactured in the United States of America

Library of Congress Cataloging in Publication Data
Swedberg, Robert W.
    American oak furniture : styles and prices : book II / Robert W.
  and Harriett Swedberg. — 2nd ed.
      p. cm.
    Includes bibliographical references and index.
    ISBN 0-87069-595-9 (hard) : — ISBN 0-87069-587-8 (pbk.)
    1. Furniture, Oak—United States—Catalogs. I. Swedberg,
  Harriett. II. Title.
  NK2405.S89   1991
  749.213'075—dc20   90-71444
                                                       CIP

1 2 3 4 5 6 7 8 9 0   9 8 7 6 5 4 3 2 1

To Pauline, Joe, Cathy, and Virl Banowetz —four
special friends of long-time standing.

Contents

Acknowledgments

The authors sincerely thank the following collectors and dealers who freely gave of their time and knowledge to assist us in obtaining photographs and prices for this book. We also thank those who did not wish to be listed.

ABC Antique Shop
Ruth Ankrom and Linda Cron
Des Moines, Iowa

An Antiques Enthusiast

Antique America
Cheryle, Lance and Norman Frye
Davenport, Iowa

Antique & Specialty Center
Colleen Higgins and Stephen Bunton
Anchorage, Alaska

Antique Emporium
Waukesha, Wisconsin

Antique Scene
Rachel Cattrell
Moline, Illinois

The Antique Shop
Napponee, Indiana

Antiques, Art 'N Treasures
Steve and Virginia Hallett
Janesville, Wisconsin

Antiques by Judy
Davenport, Iowa

Antiques et cetera
Dale and Jennie Rylander
Altona, Illinois

Banowetz Antiques
Virl and Cathy Banowetz
Maquoketa, Iowa

Beaumont House Antiques
Jim and Fawna Radewan
Rochester, Wisconsin

Beecham's Antiques
Sue and Randy Beecham
Glasford, Illinois

Blind Justice Antiques
Richard Lee
Superior, Wisconsin

Stephen and Carol Bond

Dennis and Laura Brennan

Buttermilk Hill Antiques
Terry and Evangeline Husk
Franklin, Pennsylvania

C. & D. Antiques
Chuck and Dee Robinson
Byron Center, Michigan

Cats 'N Dogs Antiques
John and Norma Beecher
West Branch, Iowa

Clarissa's Collections
Clarissa O. Koehn
Elgin, Illinois

Collector's Cupboard
Waukesha, Wisconsin

The Coopers
Jane and Florence
Marion, Iowa

Country Collectibles
Joan W. McCall
Kent, Connecticut

Cubbyhole Antiques
Bev Froelinger
Erie, Illinois

Culligan's Collection
Kathy Culligan
Arvada, Colorado

Mary Davin's Antiques
Iowa City, Iowa

Day's Past Antiques
Gary E. Hale
Breese, Illinois

Dim Lantern Antiques
Arlene Harrington
Franklin, Pennsylvania

Farm House Antiques
David and Edna Brown
Alexis, Illinois

Flowerland Nursery
Craig and Eric Johnson
Prophetstown, Illinois

Gloria and Gale Flynn

Forgotten Treasures
Cheryl and Terry Walker
Rockford, Illinois

Fort Lancaster Antiques
Mike and Sharon Naylor
Glasford, Illinois

Foxy's Antiques
E. Lenore "Foxy" Hawpe
Denver, Colorado

G. & G. Antiques
Virginia and Betty
Newton, Iowa

Mr. and Mrs. Edward Gabrys

Garland's Antiques
Garland Miller at Rocky's Antique Mall
Weyers Cave, Virginia

The Grainery Antiques
Shirley and Syd Waggoner
Fort Wayne, Indiana

Grand River Merchants Antique Mall
George and Gloria VanDusen
Williamston, Michigan

Greenwood General Store
Sharon Lord, dealer;
Mary Little, proprietor
Greenwood, Indiana

Haygood House
Watkinsville, Georgia

Nina and Chip Heffren

Marjorie Herman

Hillside Antiques
Estelle Holloway
Frankfort, Illinois

Hoss's Antiques
Pat, Hoss, and Denise Davie
Denver, Colorado

House of Bargains
Andy and Pat Baysingar
Kewanee, Illinois

House of Stuff 'N Things
Anna Figg
Buffalo, Iowa

Illinois Antique Center
Dan and Kim Philips
Peoria, Illinois

Virginia Jensen

Ken's Antiques and Collectibles
Kenneth Kite at Rocky's Antiques Mall
Weyers Cave, Virginia

Shirley Kilgard

Marc and Mona Klarman

LaMere - Brightview
Leslee and Duane LaMere
Evelyn and Owen Maxwell
Moline, Illinois

Laub's Loft
Myron and Marge Laub
Neponset, Illinois

Darlene and Walter Laud

Laura Renee Antique and Collectibles
Ben, Ellie, and Laura Goossen
Antique Emporium
Arvada, Colorado

Lionwood Antiques
Charles W. Hilliard
Bath, Ohio

Linda Lusk
Dunlap, Illinois

The Louisville Antique Mall
Harold L., Chuck and Don Sego
Louisville, Kentucky

McClaskey Antiques
Don and Mary
Burlington, Iowa

Sam and Lawanna McClure

W.D. McDonald
Columbia Antique Mall
Columbia, South Carolina

Maison Nanette
Bed and breakfast accommodations, antiques
Nanette Wayer
Anchorage, Alaska

Marley's Antiques
Marlene and Dick Faust
Oshkosh, Wisconsin

Mary Rachel Antiques
Mary Levery
Washington, Illinois

Mrs. Rosalie Mehall

Melon City Antique Mart
Joe and Mary Cline
Muscatine, Iowa

Mike's Antiques
Mike and Jane Cheer
Arvada Antique Emporium II
Arvada, Colorado

Miska's Antique Workshop
Joe Miska
Rocky's Antique Mall
Weyers Cave, Virginia

Linda and Jeffrey Moyer

My Grandmothers
Tommy L. Douglas and Richard E. Kruger
Janesville, Wisconsin

Nana's Front Room Antiques
Kathleen Constable
New Market, Maryland

Odds 'n' Ends
Lida M. Hale
Vandalia, Illinois

Old Evansville Antique Mall
Ed Small
Evansville, Indiana

Old Village Antiques
Joyce L. Ingram
Williamston, Michigan

Richard and Pat Olson
Muskego, Wisconsin

Sharon and Dick Olson

John Onken & Bro.
Clyde and Harriett Werries
Alex and Mary Lois Lacy
Chapin, Illinois

Our Town Shoppe
Marlene Lehr
Milburn, Illinois

Paris Mall
English Cap Antiques - Gary Shriver
Paris, Illinois

Paris Mall
Garry Vaughn
Paris, Illinois

Patricia Hayes Antiques
Bittersweet Shop
Gaylordsville, Connecticut

Pick's Antiques
Allen Edwards and Loren Randle
Sparland, Illinois

Pine Cupboard Antiques
L. E. Morin
Elgin, Illinois

Plain & Fancy Antiques
Mildred M. Bark
Franklin, Pennsylvania

Plaza Antique Mall
Patricia Zwyghuizen
Grand Rapids, Michigan

Pleasant Hill Antique Mall & Tea Room
Bob and Eileen Johnson
East Peoria, Illinois

Poor Richard's Antiques
Richard and Karen Melton
Spooner, Wisconsin

Putnam Street Antiques
Tim Thompson and Gordon Bloomer
Williamston, Michigan

Raccoon Hollow Antiques
Chuck and Cindy Kleckner
Freeport, Illinois

Realty and Auction Service
John A. Whalen
Neapolis, Ohio

Re: Antiques
Nancy Kennedy
Iowa City, Iowa

Red Apples Antiques
Don and Alice Strube
Milwaukee, Wisconsin

Red Barn Antiques
Rhea Heppner
Chippewa Falls, Wisconsin

Clark and Carolyn Reed

Walt and Esther Rickertsen

Ricklef's Antiques
Eloise and Doug
Anamosa, Iowa

Robbie's Antiques
Earle and Betty Robison
Lewisburg, Ohio

Deb and Randy Robison

Rocky's Antique Mall
Rocky Simonetti
Weyers Cave, Virginia

Ginger Roper
Columbia Antique Mall
Columbia, South Carolina

School Days Mall
Judy and Eric Sewell
Sturtevant, Wisconsin

Dan, Shirley, Jim, and Jennifer Shaffer

Sharron's Antiques
Steve and Sharron
Hartford, Wisconsin

Norval and Nedra Smith

Snyder's Antiques
Canton, Ohio

Joseph and Gen Sonneville

Warren K. Sparks

Stocker's Antiques
Orion, Illinois

The Trader's Post
Mary and Ski Rozanski
Golden, Colorado

Trunks 'N' Treasures
Mel and Terri Hall
Davenport, Iowa

E. Ulrich Antiques
Betty and Elmer
Roanoke, Illinois

John and Denise Van Berkum

Denny and Judy Waddell

West Rhoades Antiques
Barb and Fred Rhoades
Arvada Antique Emporium II
Arvada, Colorado

Shirley and Marvin Williams

Win's What-Nots
Gisela Schroeder
Cullom, Illinois

1   Reflections on Prices

For the first edition, the Swedbergs traveled over 12,000 miles, not including visits to local antiques shops, shows, and flea markets. Their quest for pictures led them from Colorado to Connecticut, from Wisconsin and Minnesota to Alabama and Georgia. For the 1991 revision they added thousands of miles, including a trip to Alaska to take photographs. Because museum pieces are not available for purchase, such photographs are not included in this book.

In this book only one price is given, the pricetag placed on the furniture as found. In addition, the state where it was photographed is indicated. Remember, a guide merely directs or points the way. Neither the authors nor the publisher assume responsibility for any losses that may be incurred as a result of using this guide.

Geographical differences

Regional preferences are reflected on the pricetags on collectible objects and an-

Painted oak washstand (paint can hide defects); 30" wide, 15" deep, 29" high; splashback 5½". In Virginia, **$175.**

tiques. Some areas of the country prefer oak over the formal, darker furniture woods and casual country styles. Where oak is appreciated, prices are up; where it is ignored, the value goes down. Usually residents in the West and Midwest are more oak oriented than Easterners, both in the North and South. Some shops in Alaska also feature oak.

Condition

Naturally a stray in search of a home is more appealing if it presents a good appearance. It has sales appeal if it can be moved into a home setting immediately. Some purchasers are attracted when a low pricetag is attached to an article. Bargain hunting buyers should be cautious if oak is painted. The top of a table or chest may be damaged in some manner. Could there be water rings under that enamel? (They're black and indicate that moisture has seeped through the finish into the wood fibers.) Following paint removal, it could take a great deal of sanding to eliminate such spots, and, since an indentation is produced if abrasion under pressure is applied to only the affected area, the whole surface must be sanded. Burns or grease spots are sometimes revealed after paint is stripped.

Are repairs necessary? Can you do them yourself or must you hire the job done? Inspect your prospective purchase well.

Marriages

Marriage is a state wherein two who are unrelated are united as one. Antiques advocates have adopted the term to describe a single article created by joining two previously separate units. A desk base, originally without a top, receives one that may complement it well. A bureau that lost its swinging mirror may be mated with another compatible one. When such unions occur and the dealer is aware of their existence, the customer should be told. Otherwise, ask

Washstand with replaced splashback and new brass pulls; 30½" wide, 15¼" deep, 29¼" high; splashback 7½". In Iowa, $295. Ash, elm, and maple chair; 40½" high. In Iowa, $85.

yourself: "Are the ornamentations on the top and base alike? Are the sizes correct with no overhang, or, conversely, skimpiness present? Do the lines of the piece vary?" For example, a vintage splasher (the back on a commode washstand) may have been replaced. Were its edges molded to match those on the base? If the stiles (upright supports) are chamfered (slanted) on the bottom piece, does the top conform? Does the appearance and width of the wood seem similar? Look and learn.

Cut-downs

The saw can be as harmful to furniture as a sharp human tongue is when it cuts down people. Transformations are common, and, if they meet the owner's needs, so be it. For example, in a recreation room, families frequently seek casual comfort. They'll prop their feet on a round oak coffee table that formerly functioned at full height in a dining room. How should a cut-down be priced? How should the cost of an altered piece be determined?

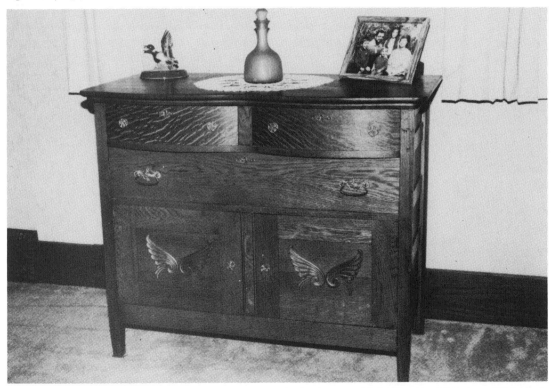

Sideboard. This is an example of a marriage candidate if a back were added; 45" wide, 22½" deep, 38" high. In Iowa, $225.

Supply and demand

Naturally, every shop proprietor tries to unite a product with a buyer. If customers don't want an article, the cash register rings up "No Sale." A piece may be rare and old, but if it does not have sales appeal, it merely occupies shop space without profiting the owner. Conversely, when the supply is limited, the demand is great, and the shop has the merchandise, that's good news.

A dealer must consider his overhead. In an urban area where walk-in trade is attracted, prices are apt to be higher because the overhead is generally greater. Rents tend to be higher. A large shop with several employees and a costlier inventory has to charge more than a small, owner-operated store in the same general locale. The cost of obtaining the merchandise must be considered. Necessary repairs must be given a dollar evaluation. Age, rarity, the expense of replacing sold objects, and the current market value are all factors that must be contemplated. Is it any wonder prices vary? As you mentally walk through this book, let your mind remind you, "It's a guide to lead me."

*Umbrella stand converted into a hanging light; 8½" square, 25" high. In Wisconsin, **$165.***

*Cut-down library table with two supporting pillars and ball feet; 36" wide, 24" deep, 19" high. In Michigan, **$495.***

2   Oak and Its Relatives

"What a lovely oak dresser," exclaimed a young woman as she wandered through an antiques shop. "I especially like the handles and the carvings."

"That's ash," the proprietor explained when he realized she might possibly purchase the piece. "The two woods resemble each other."

"Why did you tell me? Why didn't you let me buy it as oak?" the woman asked.

The dealer responded that it was not his policy to misrepresent his merchandise. He wanted his customers to return. His candor converted the young woman into a steady client.

Today, oak, an enigma, is the pampered pet of many. Oak is a puzzle because it has contrasting characteristics. It is hard and heavy, yet, despite its strength, it cracks easily. Because of this, baseball bats are made of the more resilient ash, which has an oak look. Oak is open grained, which means it has large pores for moisture absorption or expulsion. This trait helps it accept stain well. Some like it light. Some like it dark. It can be a mellow, golden color, stained, or deeply fumed with vapors.

Oak is old, yet of this century too. It was used hundreds and hundreds of years ago. It lost its popularity for a period of time when brown walnut and reddish mahogany took turns reigning. After America's virgin walnut forests were depleted (about 1880) and light, not dark furnishings received Dame Fashion's nod, oak dominated once again.

Remember, of course, that the use of oak with its look-alikes did not stop suddenly and then start again. Even when walnut was in style, oak and its sister woods, while not predominant, continued to be utilized. For example, in 1876, Grand Rapids, Michigan, was still the furniture capital of the United States. A catalog distributed from there advertised chamber (bedroom) suites in ash or walnut. An inexpensive walnut set cost twenty-seven dollars and fifty cents while the ash version sold for only twenty-three seventy-five, a difference of three seventy-five. This was during the final stages of the Victorian period when both the aging Queen Victoria, who reigned over the British Empire for slightly more than sixty-three years (1837-1901), and the styles named for her were growing wan and weary. In general, lighter, less ponderous furniture assumed the lead as the 1800s receded into history.

Oak can be plain or fancy. Although its tough surface is not easy to carve, some chairs, tables, chests, and cabinets have elaborate designs. Oak was popular in the Jacobean period, about 1603 to 1688, when furniture with ornamental carvings, twist turnings, and crestings prevailed. This style was revived briefly in the 1870s, but was not widely received. By 1900, on through the 1920s, golden oak, which had decorative features, and sturdy, stoic Mission, with its straight-slat appearance, vied for the homemaker's attention.

Elm dresser with applied decorations at top of frame; 42" wide, 20" deep, 79" high. In Alaska, **$495.**

Ash dresser, with walnut veneer panels on the drawers and a marble insert, is an example of Victorian manufacture; 37" wide, 17" deep, 39" high. In Illinois, $345.

Combination bookcase-desk with etched designs on convex glass door front, two mirrors and applied decorations; 37" wide, 12" deep, 75" high. In Iowa, $1,295.

Oak Jacobean revival-style chair, late 1870s, with Flemish spiral or twist turnings and a carved animal crest; 42½" high. In Iowa, $475.

The carved lion's head and French paw foot are seen on a china buffet from the turn of the century, golden oak era; 27¼" high from head to foot.

5

Mission-style fall-front parlor desk; 28" wide, 17" deep, 40" high. In Michigan, **$295.**

At times the decorations on golden oak were not carved into the wood. Instead, a metal die (with an engraved design) was used to machine-stamp a pattern that emulated carving. Steam aided in shaping parts. Heat, plus extreme pressure, and the quality of the design of the die itself helped to determine whether a carved look was actually achieved. Ordinarily, the impressions were shallow, not the deep decorations produced by actual cutting. When chiseling or cutting was added to the pressed design, a more deeply embossed (raised) effect was created.

Today, when collectors speak of "pressed back chairs" they are describing chairs with decorative back panels that were made by dies that molded the wood fibers. Catalogs from the past preferred the term "carved" when describing such details.

There were other methods used to give oak a dressed-up appearance. Decorations such as leaves, clusters of fruits, complicated heads, or other ornamentation could be crafted separately and then attached to the surface of furniture. These applied carvings are attractive to many who appreciate oak.

Cane seat pressed-back chair, 39" high. In Iowa, **$695** *for a set of six.*

Oak pressed-back chair with some hand carving has a pressed cane seat and French front legs; 38" high. In Wisconsin, **$125.**

Fall-front secretary with applied decorations; 42" wide, 19" deep, 81" high. In Iowa, **$1,085.**

Ice box with brass plaque reading "New Iceberg" and lift-lid ice compartment; 31" wide, 21" deep, 45" high. In Iowa, **$750.**

Oak can have calm stripes and V's or wild flakes, depending on the manner in which it is sawed into planks. When it is plain sawed, the boards are sliced lengthwise from the whole log in parallel cuts, and stripes and elliptical V's appear.

Quarter-sawed oak is created by splitting a log in half lengthwise. Each half is then cut in half. Roughly, this forms four equal triangles that are sliced into parallel boards almost at right angles to the annual growth rings. Lines called medullary or pith rays, which radiate from the center of the tree trunk, are then exposed. In oak, these rays are so defined they are referred to as flakes. They are the largest found in any native American tree. While quarter sawing increases the cost because wood is wasted and extra processing is necessary, it does have advantages. The resulting product shrinks and warps less than plain sawed wood does, and the pattern is more vivid.

Did you know that oak trees can live two or three hundred years, and some add centuries to that time limit? They seem to shudder and shiver and do not select severely cold areas as their native habitat. There are approximately two hundred and seventy-five known varieties of these trees rooted around the world. Of this amazing number, about sixty varieties are found in the United States.

Approximately fourteen are consistently utilized by the home furnishing industry. In this country, white oak, with its combination of strength, beauty, and durability, is the primary choice. Oak has another endearing trait. It is slow to rot, so it is less apt to suffer damage when stored in a damp basement or when subjected to alternately wet and dry conditions. That's a true plus.

Oak has emulators. It almost becomes a sextet, because ash, chestnut (much of which was destroyed by a blight in the early 1900s), elm, and hickory produce lumber with an appearance very similar to oak. Add another, a faker — artificial oak graining. Less expensive light woods were stroked with color applied with special rollers or combs, brushes, and even rags or crumpled paper. This bit of hanky-panky created a less expensive product that was appealing to those who liked to follow modern trends but could not afford to pay the price current in 1897 of sixteen dollars for an "elegant solid oak bedroom suite." Instead, they could purchase a similar set "finished very handsomely in antique oak," the base wood not specified, from the *Sears Roebuck Catalogue*, for ten dollars and fifty cents. Hotels frequently found such bargains attractive.

Recently a couple bought an extension table with a battered finish that they stripped off. The "oak" on the top and on the legs slid away as the paint remover began to act. The artificial grain went down the drain. Alas, only the apron was oak, but the table with its mixed light woods proved to be attractive anyhow.

The following chart lists the various traits of a tree sextet comprised of oak and its five emulators.

Oak sewing cabinet with panels constructed of quarter-sawn oak showing its characteristic medullary or pith rays, which appear as vivid flakes, is enhanced by twisted pilasters, beading, and applied decorations; 24½" wide, 20" deep, 31" high. In Illinois, $195.

Artificially grained oak chiffonier; 34" wide, 18" deep, 48" high. In Alaska, $350.

Characteristics of oak and its look-alikes

Tree	General color	Approximate dates used	Characteristics and main uses
Ash	grayish to creamy	1875-1925. Victorian furniture advertised c. 1875 was available in ash or walnut. Ash was found during the oak period, through the early 1900s.	Grain resembles oak. Strong. Used for furniture including upholstery frames where strength is required. Shovel, hoe, and rake handles; oars; tennis racquets; skis; baseball bats (oak bats tend to crack) are other items made of ash. Bends well for hoops and bow backs on chairs. Entire bedroom sets were available in ash in the 1870s. Many "oak" iceboxes are really ash.
Chestnut	grayish brown	mainly early 1900s	Has coarse, open grain, but lacks the large rays; is softer and not as structurally tough as oak. Frequently used for drawer construction and as core (base) for veneer. Resists warping. Used for picture frames, woodwork, and paneling. Blight hit wild trees in early 1900s, destroying most of this country's supply.
Elm	very light brown	early 1900s	Porous with an oaklike texture. Since it bends easily and does not split readily, it is suitable for curved parts in furniture, such as hoop backs on chairs. Used extensively today for decorative veneers because of its pleasing figure. Elm tends to warp and this is curbed when it is applied as veneer over another surface. Many so-called "oak" iceboxes are actually elm.
Hickory	tan	early 1900s	Has oak color and texture. Strong, supple, tough, splintery, hard-to-work. Good for furniture parts where strength and thinness are both essential. Used for larger bent pieces in colonial furniture. Foremost wood for tool handles.
Oak	white to yellow	Revival of oak about 1890-1925, but oak was used extensively prior to 1700. Jacobean styles, 1603-1688, favored oak. Except for minor revivals, oak was out of fashion until the late 1800s.	Oak is light in color, heavy, hard, coarse, durable, with large pores. Very distinct pith or medullary rays (called flakes), the largest rays in any native American tree, show in the quarter-sawed lumber. When plain sawed, elliptical V's often are seen.
Artificial grain	oak look	late 1800s, early 1900s	A fake oak grain could be applied to inexpensive woods that had little or no pattern. Small hotels or families of modest means, who desired to be fashionable, could decorate with artificially grained furniture very economically.

Please turn to the Glossary at the back of the book for definitions of terms used. Oak and its resemblers are all open-grained woods. This means there are small pores or openings in the wood through which fluids are absorbed and discharged. When these can be seen readily, the wood is called open-grained. Closed-grain wood has pores that are difficult to distinguish.

All are hardwoods. They come from deciduous (leaf-shedding) trees with broad leaves, in contrast to evergreens, which provide soft lumber and are needle-bearing conifers (have cones).

Oak and its look-alikes have all been used in some aspect in the furniture industry. Oak is ranked as a leading American furniture wood.

How to detect artificial graining

On a stand or table, check underneath the top to see whether the pattern has similar characteristics on both the top and bottom. On case pieces such as dressers and desks, inspect the inside of a solid wood (not veneered) drawer front and note whether the outside resembles it. Or remove the first drawer and look underneath the top to see if the two sides match each other. Frequently pale and worn spots will be present from constant touching around drawer pulls or on the surface where objects were moved about. Most fake graining will dissolve in the solvent if refinishing is attempted.

Just think, many of you are now smarter than the average antiquer. You are aware that there are five other woods that may easily be mistaken for oak. The wood species will not be designated under the pictures in the chapters that follow, but now you know there are differences.

Ash commode washstand; 35" wide, 21" deep, 34" high. In Michigan, **$330.**

Ash ice box; 30" wide, 18" deep, 48" high. In Illinois, $495.

Elm swivel desk chair that tilts and revolves with cane seat; 24" arm to arm, 46½" high. In Illinois, $450.

Swivel desk chair that tilts and revolves, made of oak, ash, maple, and elm for bending; 21" arm to arm, 45½" high. In Iowa, $425.

Elm dresser with swing mirror; 42" wide, 21" deep, 74" high. In Illinois, $350.

Factory stamp found on the back of elm dresser.

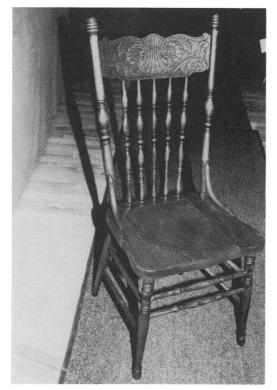

*Elm pressed-back chair; 41" high. In Wisconsin, one of a set of four, **$225** each.*

*Oak tilt-back cane chair with coil springs; hickory is used on the bent part where strength is essential; 21½" arm to arm, 35" high. In Iowa, **$325.***

Oak sideboard in quarter-sawed oak; 48" wide, 20" deep, 52" high. In Illinois, **$495.**

Oak-ash two-piece cupboard; 38" wide, 16½" deep, 83" high. In Indiana, **$725.**

Quarter-sawed oak top and maple-legged extension table with center leg support and five leaves; 45" square, 30" high. In Alaska, **$950.**

Artificially grained collapsible or breakdown wardrobe with two drawers at base; 48" wide, 17" deep, 86" high. In Illinois, **$795.**

Elm and maple youth chair, 44" high. In Michigan, **$95.**

Ash and selected hardwood cradle; 38" wide, 22" deep, 31" high. In Michigan, **$345.**

Spit and polish is a term that describes the military precision of overly emphasized orderliness. It was spit that inspired David W. Kendall, one of the first furniture designers in Grand Rapids, Michigan. The Phoenix Furniture Company hired him in 1879, and their choice was wise, because he assumed a position of creative leadership in his field. Kendall designed a squared bed headboard to compete with the high arches and circles in vogue at that time and experimented with decorative touches not related to carving, including metal ornamentation. He copied period styles that he saw and studied in England. Walnut was becoming scarce, but oak, with its tendency to be hard to work and lighter in color than he desired, was readily available.

In the company's factory, the floors were made of oak. Workers who chewed tobacco were not always accurate when they aimed the residue from their bulging cheeks. Sometimes they hit the spittoons. Frequently they missed. If it landed on the floor, so what?

Kendall observed that the wood had become darkened from the tobacco stains. The resulting brown reminded him of patina, the natural aging process that deepens the color of wood after years of exposure to light, air, and dirt. He experimented with a concoction containing chewing tobacco to deepen oak's pale tone and was pleased with its appearance. However, the finish was not endurable. Kendall persisted and learned to use chemicals to achieve the characteristics he sought. His cynical competitors called it "mud," but they stopped smirking and quickly imitated his product when they noted its sales appeal. Besides genuine oak, elm, and ash, other hardwoods were soon disguised as antique oak. Kendall's recognition of the effect of tobacco expectorations on wood helped him create a new, marketable product.

Now for the polish portion of spit and polish. Many people, then as now, preferred their oak light, so a glossy, golden tone captured the number one position in popularity in the early years of this century. This furniture was frequently described as being "highly polished" or as possessing a "high gloss golden finish." A finish helps preserve and polish wood and enhance its beauty, but mainly it is a necessity to help protect the surface from damage. (For example, varnish is used as a durable coating. Moisture from a damp glass set on unprotected wood might penetrate the fibers and cause a black ring to form. While moisture can and does seep through finishes, the varnish retards the process.)

When dark walnut and mahogany departed and the heavy drapes and the excessive bric-a-brac the Victorians adored was stored away, golden oak bowed into the scene at center stage. Golden oak — what a glittering name for a finish that was frequently produced by simply applying orange shellac to the wood. Sometimes yellow pigments might also be added to capture a sunshiny, Midas touch. Advertisements published in 1908 stated, however, that the gold in the wood was brought up through repeated applications of the best grade of varnish.

Grand Rapids, Michigan, was a major furniture manufacturing center until after WWII. The earliest mention of golden oak at a Grand Rapids library was 1890. The Manistee Manufacturing Company in Manistee advertised a massive golden oak sideboard for fourteen dollars. In 1895, the Widdicomb Furniture Company of Grand Rapids was offering bedchamber and dining room suites in white oak, golden oak, birch, and mahogany. Around 1900, plain, slatted, Mission oak, with its deep, "fumed" surface, was introduced on the market. Many types, styles, and finishes of oak furniture vied for consumer attention at the turn of the century.

The golden oak period, which lasted from about 1890 through the late 1920s, will be considered first.

3   The Welcoming Hall

*Hall tree with lift-lid storage compartment, brass drip pan, and applied decorations; 35" arm to arm, 17" deep, 78½" high. In Iowa, **$1,795**.*

A first impression is important, and, in former years, many homes had entrance halls where guests were greeted and given a preview of the home's decor. Like people, halls came in different sizes and shapes. They could be Jack Spratt narrow and long and afford access to various doorways or to an ascending staircase. They might be wide like Jack Spratt's wife, almost large enough to appear room size, especially when the house was designed for someone who was more affluent than average. In such hallways, ornamental furniture welcomed guests and presented a dramatic impression of how the family lived.

The utilitarian hall tree was customarily present and provided a place to hang hats or coats. Often it included a bench with a hinged lid. There, overshoes, which were made of rubber, could be hidden from sight and out from underfoot. Some hall trees had circular arms that embraced collapsed, dripping umbrellas. Rainwater was safely drained into drip pans, many of which lent themselves to ornamentation such as the shell-shaped metal containers pictured. A mirror was a necessary part of these stands. Here a hat could be adjusted before leaving the house. Conversely, upon entering, a blown coiffure could be patted back into place or a stray bit of hair could be tucked in before a guest made an appearance. Stands that were top-heavy were secured to the wall for stability.

For a decidedly eye-engaging entrance, a giant hall tree would demand a spacious area. Notice the features of the one pictured. It has a beveled mirror surrounded by a narrow edging of beaded molding. The frame itself is graced with embossed leaves and scrolls. Two massive, carved, imaginary animals form the arms of the boxed base, with its hinged storage enhanced with sunken, molded panels, carving, and beading. The figures have the head, mane, and feet of an animal, exotic wings, and a dragon-type tail. Such a fantastic creation is called a chimera or

Hall tree with lift-lid storage compartment, ornate leaf carving, brass hat hooks, and carved imaginary animals called chimeras (*wild beasts of the imagination*) *that form the arms; 54½" wide, 20½" deep, 89" high. In Illinois,* **$3,500.**

Hall tree with lift-lid storage compartment; 36" arm to arm, 15½" deep, 81" high. In Wisconsin, **$1,095.**

chimaera. They are mythological in origin, evolving from a fire-breathing monster that possessed a lion head, a shaggy goat body, and a tail. In simplest terms, chimeras may be defined as horrible creatures of the imagination. Two terms that do not fit, according to traditional definition, are gargoyle and griffin. A gargoyle originally was a grotesquely carved waterspout that projected from the gutter of a building. It could be any fantastic architectural creature with an extended outward thrust. While it is not strictly correct to call similar appendages on furniture by this name, it is heard. The term griffin is used when referring to another imaginary animal possessing the forepart of an eagle with wings spread and claw feet ready to pounce on its prey combined with the haunches and tail of a lion. It's correct to refer to bizarre designs of people or animals, either partial or whole forms, as grotesques, a term that encompasses many fantastic figures. Whatever you call the arms, this ornate hall tree would indeed constitute a memorable furnishing in an entryway.

Close-up of chimera (a wild beast of the imagination) on hall tree. (See text for explanation.)

Here are some decorative features used on golden oak. As has been stated previously:

grotesques are figures or parts of figures of animals and people mixed with flowers, fruits, or foliage created in a fantastic or unnatural way.

chimera or chimaera, according to Greek mythology, is a fire breathing creature with a lion's head, a goats's body, and a serpent's tail. In more general terms it can be simply defined as a horrible creature of the imagination.

finial is a decorative end for a post or pediment.

fretwork is cut-out ornamental work that is interlocking in design.

Fretwork from an old home. In Colorado, **$340.**

Sideboard with applied decorations and grotesques on base doors and on top rail; 56" wide, 25" deep, 82" high. In Illinois, **$1,995.**

18

Grotesque on desk fall front.

Grotesque on the rail of a chair.

19

Grotesque on the cornice of a combination bookcase-desk.

Grotesque on fall front of a combination bookcase-desk.

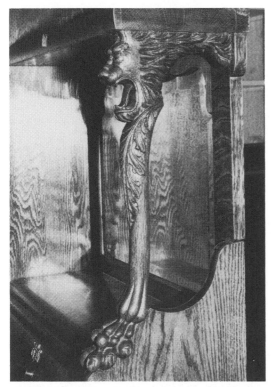

Grotesque used as a shelf support on a combination bookcase-desk.

Grotesque applied to the pilaster in the bookcase section of a combination bookcase-desk.

20

Male finial on the right back post of an upholstered chair.

Grotesque between the front legs of an upholstered armchair.

Hall tree with lift lid, four hat and coat hooks, mirror and applied decorations; 29" wide, 16" deep, 78" high. In Iowa, **$1,190.**

Hall tree with lift-lid storage compartment, brass hat hooks, inverted heart design, and applied decorations; 25½" arm to arm, 17½" deep, 77" high. In Illinois, **$950.**

Hall tree with lift-lid storage compartment, brass hat hooks, applied decorations, and shell design at crest; 33" wide, 17" deep, 84" high. In Illinois, **$875.**

Hall tree with lift-lid storage compartment (sometimes listed in early catalogues as a ''lid to seat for rubbers'' or ''to hold rubbers, etc.'') 29" arm to arm, 16" deep, 78½" high. In Iowa, **$895.**

Icebox with brass plaque reading, "'Success' Huene-feld Co., Cincinnati, Ohio''; 26" wide, 18" deep, 43" high. In Indiana, **$485.**

China cabinet with convex glass in side panels and in central door, pillars, leaded and beveled glass panels near top, applied decorations and paw feet; 47" wide, 17" deep, 76" high. In Texas, **$2,250.**

Morris chair with incised carving on front legs and apron and grotesques on arm ends; 30" arm to arm, 31" high. In Alaska, **$595.**

Sideboard with swell top drawers, two paneled base drawers, applied decorations and paw feet; 60" wide, 25" deep, 67" high. In Kentucky, **$995.**

Ash commode washstand with applied decorations, mirror and attached towel bar; 33" wide, 18" deep, 72" high. In Wisconsin, **$495.**

Cheval dresser with applied drawer panels and incised decorations; 41" wide, 20" deep, 77" high. In Illinois, $665.

Hoosier-type cupboard with sugar and flour bins and pull-out cutting board; 42" wide, 26" deep, 73" high. In Illinois, $795.

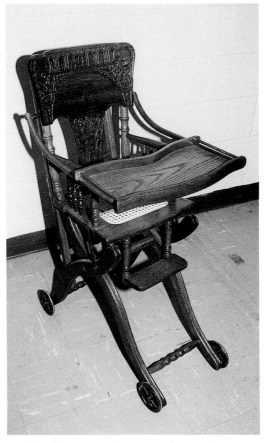

Highchair/go-cart combination with pressed cane seat and pressed design on back and splat; 18" wide, 38" high. In Wisconsin, **$495.**

Chiffonier (highboy) with hatbox compartment; 43" wide, 18" deep, 53" high. In Illinois, **$395.**

*Lady's or parlor fall-front desk with one drawer, door and two shelves above drop lid; one drawer and two shelves below; and applied and incised decorations; 30" wide, 17" deep, 60" high. In Ohio, **$1,300.***

*Ash two-piece cylinder secretary with burl walnut on cylinder front and incised decorations; 24" wide, 21" deep, 91" high. In Iowa, **$2,950.***

Bed with applied decorations on head- and foot-boards; 58½" wide, 78¼" long, 82" high at head-board. In Iowa, **$550.**

Table; 42" square, 28" high with three 9½" leaves. In Illinois, **$395.** *Cane seat chairs with pressed-back design; 38½" high;* **$80** *each. One-piece stepback cupboard; 43½" wide, 22¼" deep, 79" high;* **$350.**

"Time Is Money" shelf clock with thermometer and level built in; 15½" wide, 5½" deep, 24" high. In Colorado, $225. Oak and walnut clock shelf; 18" wide, 6¼" deep, 8½" high; $65.

Folding screen; each panel 17½" wide, 55" high. In Iowa, $210. Plant or lamp table; 16" square, 29" high; $155. Phonograph; 13" wide, 14½" deep, 7¼" high; $250.

Brass, marble, and oak shoe shine stand from Dallas, Texas; 22" wide, 36" deep, 62" high. In Colorado, **$750.** *Wooden barber pole from Maine; 75" high;* **$350.** *Barber sign; 18" diameter, 8" deep;* **$275.** *Three-station, marble top barbership backbar;* **$3,500.**

Architecturally speaking, the wall space between windows and other openings is referred to as a pier. When a looking glass (usually long and narrow) was placed in such a location, it was called a pier mirror. Sometimes it was hung over a table. These mirrors could occupy other narrow spots and are still used in halls today. A family with less opulent quarters might be content with a smaller mirror equipped with hooks for hats.

Hall tree with two hat and coat hooks and applied decorations; 28" wide, 18" deep, 77" high. In Michigan, **$525.**

Pier mirror with ball and stick designs and mahogany pillars; 26" wide, 10" deep, 94" high. In Iowa, **$995.**

Hall mirror with hat hooks, beading, and applied decoration; 33" × 33". In Iowa, **$250.**

Hall mirror with iron hat hooks; 29″ × 19″. In Wisconsin, **$175.**

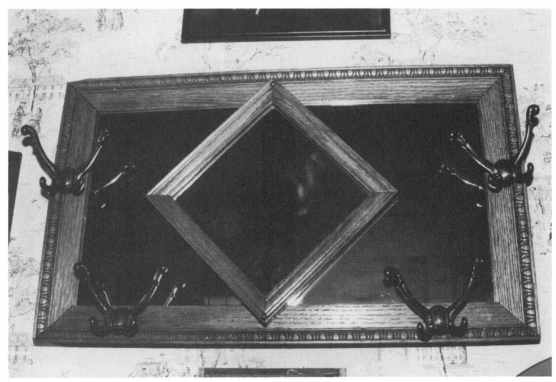

Double hall mirror with iron hat hooks; 26″ × 15¼″. In Iowa, **$325.**

*Hall mirror with ogee frame and four corner hat hooks; 42" wide, 32" high. In Iowa, **$275.***

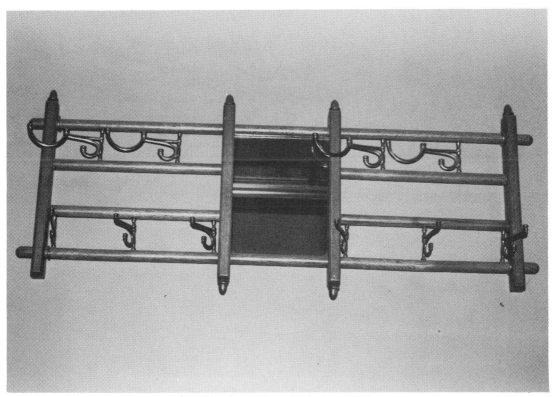

*Hat rack with mirror and ten brass swivel hooks; 35¹/₂" × 15". In Iowa, **$165.***

Roman chair with scooped seat; 25" arm to arm, 38" high. In Iowa, **$345.**

But that's not all that was in a hall, especially one of generous size. Ornamental seats might be assigned to such an area. While these could also lend the parlor a dignified air, they were called reception chairs. A paper label on the base of one illustrated chair states that it was manufactured by the Michigan Chair Company. A grotesque head with some piercing is carved into the narrow back. The position of the legs would suggest that it could be backed into a corner with ease.

A Roman chair, nicely designed for the hall, reception room, or parlor, features a curved, scooped-out seat. Predecessors of this chair have been preserved from the Italian Renaissance period, but, while there is some resemblance, the ancient versions folded and the bases were x-shaped.

A round seat was combined with a rectangular back with a tavern-type scene in bas relief to create a fancy chair. Such a piece usually would not be found in the average home.

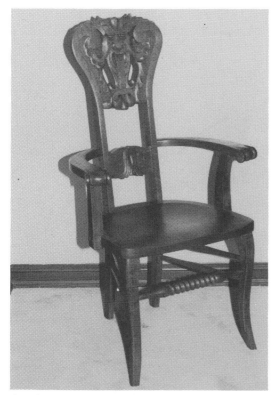

Armchair with intricately carved head; 22¼" arm to arm, 41½" high. In Illinois, **$275.**

Close-up of intricately carved chair back, called gro-tesque; *13¼" wide, 12" high.*

The bench is unusual, with its precisely embossed carvings of angel-like creatures around an urn. The top of the seat has faces on it. Notice the bentwood frame. Windsor chairs, especially in the 1700s, made use of wet wood forced into bows for backs and held firmly in that position until the wood dried into shape. The work of Michael Thonet of Vienna, Austria, was different. He signed and mass-produced light, strong, aesthetically pleasing furniture constructed from steam-bent wooden rods. He began creating furniture in about 1840 and his ideas were spread through international exhibitions where his works were shown. Thonet-type furniture has been made ever since. Durability without heaviness is one of its chief attributes, and this bench follows that concept.

Interior designers declare that the hall sets the theme for the home. If it is intriguing and attractive, it entices guests to explore and enjoy the decor further. Here too are mirrors where guests or family can primp a bit. A seat where outside footwear can be donned in comfort and a place to set things while entering or leaving are graciously added assets. Yes, the hall of a home does set the tone. So — come on in!

Chair with carved tavern scene on back; 18" × 19" back, 35½" high. In Illinois, $375.

Bench with bentwood frame, embossed, angel-like creatures on back, and two horns and faces (which cannot be seen) on seat. In Iowa, $850.

4   The Stylish Parlor

When guests accept an invitation into a parlor, they expect some form of comfortable seating to be available. Rocking chairs with their gentle, swaying movement have always lured sitters. In the past, tradition decreed that males have man-sized, large rockers with arms, while the ladies were assigned daintier versions, usually without arms. Perhaps in the late 1800s and early 1900s it was easier to settle the long, full skirts in an open seat. Maybe it was handier to hold a nursing infant or to manipulate sewing, knitting, or crocheting while seated in an armless chair. In the kitchen, sitting with a basket or pan on the lap while stringing beans, shelling garden-fresh peas, or peeling potatoes for the pot or apples for deep, rich pies might have seemed easier in such a rocker. There may have been other reasons besides the size of the occupant and price considerations that differentiated the male from the female rocker.

Notice how lightly the design is pressed into the back top rail of the first two rockers shown. Compare these to examples following, with their precise designs. Hand cutting with a knife or chisel may have been used to make the ornamentation stand out in a deeply embossed fashion.

Cane seat lady's rocker; 39" high. In Illinois, $210.

Cane seat ash rocker with sheaf of wheat impressed in top rail; 26" arm to arm, 43½" high. In Iowa, $345.

Veneer is a thin slice of a more decorative, rare, or expensive wood glued over the surface of a base that is usually less desirable. When an ornamental species is fragile, gluing it over a core gives it strength. Pictured is a rocker with a veneered seat with a roll, which is easier to achieve in a thin slice than in solid wood. Backs, too, could be veneered.

Lady's pressed-back rocker; 38" high. In Illinois, **$165.**

Rocker with pressed and carved lions' heads on back supports; 27" arm to arm, 36½" high. In Wisconsin, **$310.**

Close-up of lion's head on upright post.

*Rocker with veneered back and rolled veneer seat; 26"
arm to arm, 35" high. In Michigan,* **$395.**

Before coil springs were invented in France
during the reign of Louis XV (1715-1774),
feathers, animal hair, or other stuffing supported
on webbing softened seats and backs of chairs.
Hair or cotton batting might be stuffed around the
metal springs. Upholstery materials used with
golden oak included plush, velour, brocaded silk,
damask, and both imitation and genuine leather.
Buttons were sewn through the fabric to tie it
down. The folds that resulted and the dimpled
spacing of the buttons created attractive patterns.
An upholstered rocker might appear ponderous,
but its generous proportions offered a haven for
weary bodies.

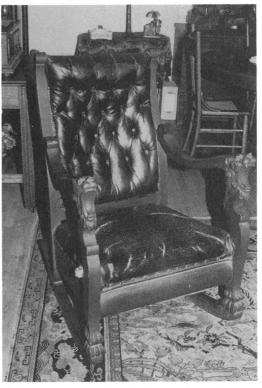

*Upholstered rocker with tufted back and carved animal
heads on arms; 27" arm to arm, 40" high. In Colorado,*
$395.

*Rocker with upholstered circle seat and finger hold in
back rail; 22" arm to arm, 36" high. In Illinois,* **$355.**

Cane seat rocker with pressed top rail and spindle back; 26" arm to arm, 41" high. In Iowa, **$265.**

Rocker with wicker curlique scrolls and upholstered seat; 24" arm to arm, 46" high. In Michigan, **$225.**

Rocker with spindle back, brass straps on top rail and upholstered seat, 44" high. In Iowa, **$125.**

Cane seat rocker with rolled arms and a pressed back in the design of a grotesque (painting, sculpture, etc., combining designs, ornaments, figures of persons, or animals in a fantastic or unnatural way); 24" arm to arm, 43" high. In Iowa, **$450.**

Close-up of grotesque on back rail of rocker.

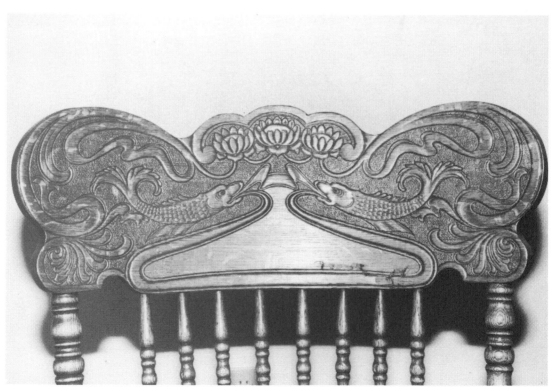

Close-up of the intricate pressed-carved design on back rail.

32

Cane seat rocker with rolled arms and a rare, fish-like, pressed-carved design on back rail; 22" arm to arm, 40½" high. In Iowa, $595.

Rocker with grotesque in pressed back; 23½" arm to arm, 37" high. In Wisconsin, $345.

Close-up of grotesque on back rail of rocker.

Close-up of man-of-the-wind pressed back.

*Rocker with man-of-the-wind pressed back; 24" arm to arm, 40" high. In Illinois, **$310.***

*Cane seat rocker with pressed-back rail; 25" arm to arm, 43" high. In Iowa, **$345.***

Close-up of animal head on rocker's arm.

Rocker with upholstered seat and grotesque carved on back panel; 25½" arm to arm, 32" high. In Illinois, $325.

In the United States, the use of chairs with legs supported on curved slats dates back to the last of the 1700s. Many such rocking chairs have a tendency to creep across the floor when someone rocks in them. The curved rockers can also cut into the carpet. There were (and are) people who feared such contrivances might tip over backwards and spill them out. Others, much to their dismay, actually rocked their way off porches. Perhaps for one or all of these reasons, inventors in the late 1800s developed various types of patented chairs that jiggled on springs or swung on bases or platforms that kept the sitter in motion, but safe. These were termed patent rockers, but the common name now is platform rocker.

Morris chair with retractable footrest and adjustable height rod in back; 29" arm to arm, 40" high. In Alaska, $595.

35

*Platform rocker with upholstered seat and back; 22"
arm to arm, 38" high. In Iowa,* **$219.**

*Platform or patent rocker with upholstered seat and
back; 29" arm to arm, 36" high. In Pennsylvania,* **$325.**

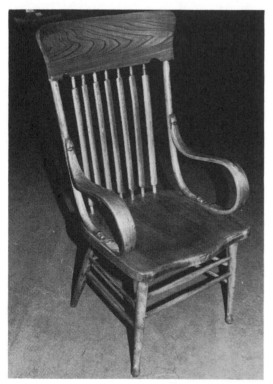

*Armchair with bentwood arms; 22" arm to arm, 43½"
high. In Illinois,* **$180.**

Straight chairs were also found in the parlor.
Plain types with arms might be a part of a dining
room suite. Those with elaborate designs or
unusual shapes customarily were not intended for
use in the eating area, especially in a home of a
family with a moderate income. Wealthy people
could have the ostentatious furnishings. Chairs
that were angled so that they could be backed into
corners were frequently elaborate in their design.

Armchair with provision for pressed cane seat or seat of your choice; 23½" arm to arm, 39" high. In Iowa, $275 each in a set of six.

Chair with upholstered seat and barrel back; 24" arm to arm, 34" high. In Michigan, $75.

Arm chair with applied decoration on top rail; 24" arm to arm, 45" high. In Iowa, $595.

Armchair with floral design on carved back and heads impressed on arms; 25½" arm to arm, 42" high. In Illinois, $375.

Corner chair with upholstered seat; 25" arm to arm, 30½" high. In Iowa, **$365.**

Arm chair with black leather seat and back; 25" arm to arm, 41" high. In Iowa, **$350.**

A Roman style with a C-shaped seat bears a vague resemblance to an Italian Renaissance chair. It could grace a corner or a window area in the parlor or could be included in a hall setting. A replica of an 1897 Sears catalog features ladies' tailor-made suits and floor-brushing skirts that are straight in front with a gathered fullness to the rear. To add to their four-and-one-half-yard sweep, they might be interlined with crinoline and lined with taffeta for a really deep flair. Benches with no backs might have accommodated all this stiffness and material more easily than a regular chair. Padding that made the skirt protrude in the derriere was a haircloth hip pad bustle. Price: fifty-six cents. Pronounced bustles were prevalent in the 1870s, but the bulge in back was gradually lessening and, by 1908, hip-form petticoats with a slight padding to the rear were advertised. The bulge was securely stitched in place and gave a woman that perfect, sought-after figure. While the bustle was hustling out of fashion during the golden oak period, there were some years when it continued to be in style. Therefore, those who dub this scooped-out seat a "bustle bench" have some basis for adopting that term.

Another seat that could accommodate a skirt of the 1900s, with its extensive yardage and dust-ruffled petticoat, was the one-armed divan. A lady could pose with one elbow on the armrest and appear alert yet comfortable. Small-sized upholstered pieces designed for more than one occupant were also classified as divans. Larger examples were called sofas. It was not unusual for living room suites to include both of these plus a platform rocker, a pair of side chairs, and a larger chair with arms. The same upholstery and identical ornamental design on the wood distinguished these groupings. Matching was very much in vogue, and parlors looked as if all of the furniture was purchased in one stop. Designers today are more likely to suggest mixing compatible types from various periods and disdain matchmaking. They prefer variety to stimulate interesting settings.

Divan with armrest and pierced carving in back; 26″ wide, 33″ high. In Colorado, $310.

Piano stool with claw and glass-ball feet; 12″ diameter, 20″ high. In Michigan, $165.

Sofa; 47″ wide, 39″ high. In Iowa, $445.

Three-piece parlor set consisting of rocker—27" arm to arm, 36" high; arm chair—27" arm to arm, 36" high; and settee or sofa—49" arm to arm, 37" high. In Iowa, **$300** *for the three-piece set.*

Two-piece parlor set consisting of platform rocker—23" arm to arm, 39" high; and loveseat—52" arm to arm, 36" high. In Iowa, **$365** *for the two-piece set.*

Mission-style sofa bed; 61" wide, 34" deep, 38" high. In Alaska, **$1,195.**

Elm rocking bench with bentwood arms; 44" wide, 36" high. In Illinois, **$425.**

Parlor table with ball-and-stick apron design; 22" square, 30" high. In Michigan, **$250.**

Parlor table with cloverleaf top, round base shelf and beading on legs; 17" wide, 29" high. In Michigan, **$245.**

Oval parlor table with carving at top of cabriole legs; 40" wide, 26" deep, 30" high. In Virginia, **$255.**

A table's reason for existence is to afford a place to set objects. In the parlor, various types of tables fulfilled different duties. In the early 1900s many homes, especially those in rural areas, were not electrified. Kerosene lamps were placed on tables. Of course, in cities where there were electric power plants, the incandescent light prevailed. During the period of transition, lamps were sometimes made on an either/or basis. They could burn kerosene or they included the necessary provisions for a rapid conversion to electric power.

The electric light celebrated its one-hundredth anniversary in 1979. On October 19, 1879, Thomas Alva Edison's incandescent bulb began to glow. By 1892, electric lights installed on the streets of one section of New York City almost seemed to recreate daylight, and people in a holiday mood celebrated the event with joyful wonder.

The Columbian Exposition in Chicago amazed those who attended it in 1893, because electric lights lit up the site. By the 1930s, the United States government was promoting rural electrification projects; thus, many parlor tables held electric lamps. Many tables had splayed (slanted out) legs, some of which terminated with glass balls held in the clutches of claw feet. A graceful French leg appeared frequently. It bowed out at the knee, curved in gently, then swept out again slightly at the foot. This double curve was called a cabriole leg and it was copied from late sixteenth century European examples. It was not unusual for carvings or applied decorations to appear on the bulging knee. Some cabriole legs had claw and ball feet.

Parlor table with claw and glass-ball feet; 29″ diameter, 29″ high. In Iowa, **$650.**

Parlor table with scalloped edges; 24″ square, 27½″ high. In Illinois, **$275.**

Couch, often called a fainting couch or chaise lounge, with stepback and applied decorations; 72″ long, 21″ deep, 34″ high. In Illinois, **$525.**

An ornate table from the late 1800s has an applied carving of a face on the apron. A close-up of the head shows the detail of this artistic work. Incised as well as applied carvings further enhance the piece. Another table from the past century was discovered in New York State. Its plain lines contrast sharply with those of the highly decorated example.

Folding tables and tilt-tops are not common in oak or its companion look-alike woods, but they did save space. Many years ago when afternoon teas were an entertainment special for the ladies, tilt-top tables were handy. They could be compacted and placed out of the way when not in use. If friends came to call, the surface could be raised to hold the refreshments. They were decorative and utilitarian. Examples of other parlor tables typical of the times are also shown.

Parlor table with pedestal base; 24" square, 30" high. In Michigan, $275.

Folding table; 24" square, 27½" high. In Illinois, $125.

Tilt-top table, which is rarely found in oak; 22" wide, 18" deep, 28" high. In Illinois, $325.

45

Parlor table with ornately carved legs, applied decoration, and carved child's head on apron; 29" wide, 16" deep, 29½" high. In Illinois, **$650.**

Close-up of child's head on apron of parlor table.

Parlor table with cloverleaf top and lower shelf; 27"
square, 29½" high. In Virginia, $245.

Plant stand; 13" square top; 33" high. In Michigan,
$145.

Plant stand; 13" diameter, 34" high. In Illinois, $135.

Pedestals were present in parlors. Plants, especially ferns with their gracefully drooping, dainty
leaves, were potted in jardinieres. (*Jardin* means
garden in French, so this is a fancy name for a
foliage holder.) Other plants or statuary of an
impressive height and nature could occupy the
surface of such stands, also. Only the round top of
the stand pictured is oak. The cabriole legs are
metal. The Italian country girl figure is made of
plaster of paris, which is often referred to as
chalkware. Fine examples were fashioned and
painted with watercolors by immigrants from Italy
who settled in the United States. They sold their
wares from approximately 1820 through the
1860s, and their efforts are usually considered to
be of a better quality than those crafted by others.
Copies of English Staffordshire porcelain and
pottery figurines were frequently made.

Short stands served as jardiniere holders, too. A
catalog advertisement of the day suggested that a
palm would look artistic if placed on one. A
taboret (or tabourette) was the name for a fancy
version. Originally this word, derived from the
French *tabour,* a small drum, referred to a low,

upholstered footstool. With the current emphasis on living foliage in home decoration, interest in stands of all heights is very strong.

Octagonal pedestal or plant stand; 12″ wide, 37″ high. In Iowa, **$100.**

Plant stand with oak top and French leg iron base; 14″ diameter, 28¼″ high. In Iowa, **$275.**

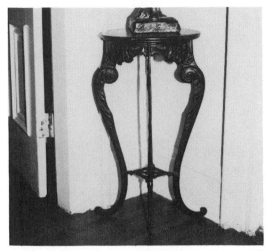

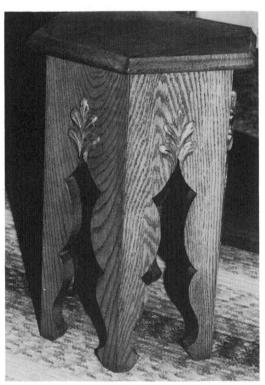

Pedestal plant stand; 14″ diameter, 36″ high. In Wisconsin, **$155.**

Taboret (or plant stand); 12″ wide, 18″ high. In Iowa, **$135.**

Pedestal plant stand; 12" diameter, 29½" high. In Illinois, **$155.**

Pedestal plant stand; 13" diameter, 34½" high. In Wisconsin, **$145.**

Pedestal plant stand; 12" diameter, 34" high. In Iowa, **$135.**

Plant stand; 12" wide, 16¼" high. In Iowa, **$75.**

Parlor table or lamp stand; 16" square, 32" high. In Wisconsin, **$225.**

Parlor table with ball-and-stick-design apron under top; 23" square, 29" high. In Wisconsin, **$245.**

Parlor table with cabriole legs and base shelf; 24" diameter, 30" high. In Michigan, **$120.**

Parlor table with glass ball and claw feet; 27" square, 29½" high. In Illinois, **$350.**

Plant stand with cabriole legs; 12" square, 18" high. In Iowa, **$165.**

Plant stand with scroll feet; 12" diameter, 18" high. In Wisconsin, **$145.**

Plant stand; 12" square top, 36" high. In Michigan, **$125.**

A display stand with bamboo posts topped by brass finials has an Oriental feel. When actual bamboo was not used in the construction, turnings that simulated it were crafted to appease the craze for styles from the Far East. These were dubbed "bamboo turnings," and when a yellow ocher was applied as a stain, a natural appearance was achieved.

Elegant homes could have music rooms, but in less pretentious dwellings, organs and music boxes were placed in the parlor.

Merchants of the late 1800s advertised that no one had to take lessons and practice hard to produce good music. Music could vibrate through the home instantly by a pull or a push or a flip of a lever, and the sounds of not merely one but many instruments could be heard. The wonder that made this possible was the music box, which was introduced in the mid-1830s.

A watchmaker in Switzerland is credited with inventing a music box in the mid-1700s. Others improved on his creation until a revolving cylinder punctuated with petite steel projecting pins

*Display stand with bamboo posts and brass finials; 17"
wide, 12" deep, 38½" high. In Wisconsin, $165.*

*Symphoniom music box with 15" disks; 24" wide, 20½"
deep. In Colorado, $3,250. Parlor table; 29½" square,
31½" high, $350.*

evolved. As it turned, the pins came into contact
with steel prongs (combs). The size and length of
each comb produced different tones of the scale,
and as the circling pins hit them, causing them to
vibrate, a melody flowed forth. The number of
tunes on a cylinder gradually increased until as
many as a dozen might be included. By the
1870s, boxes were available that permitted cylinders to be interchanged so that more melodies
could be played.

When disks were developed that could be put on
or removed much as records are switched today,
innumerable airs were available to purchasers.
Paper cylinders that resembled those found in
player pianos were used in later boxes. At first,
many machines, including the Symphoniom, were
imported from Germany. The Regina, introduced
in the 1890s and made at Rahway, New Jersey, was
the first music box manufactured in the United
States. Each Regina was numbered. Today, it is not
unusual to read ads in antiques periodicals that
invite collectors to send in the Regina model
number and receive, for a small fee, the name of
the original buyer and the year of purchase. After
making over eighty thousand Reginas, the factory
closed in 1917. The Capitol was also a well-known
version created in America.

*Coin-operated Regina music box with cylinders; 24"
wide, 17" deep, 49" high. In Iowa, $4,695.*

One major cause for the decline in music box sales was the invention of the phonograph by Thomas A. Edison in 1877. Many companies, basing their "talking machines" on Edison's, helped the new industry evolve. As the 1800s drew to a close, combination music box-phonographs, including the Reginaphone, became available. By the beginning of the twentieth century, the popularity of the phonograph was well established.

You could tell that Edison was a father. How else would he be able to recite the nursery rhyme "Mary Had a Little Lamb" so that the first tinfoil-covered cylinder repeated the words back to him? When this occurred, he and his shop foreman were both surprised and pleased, and, of all his one thousand, one-hundred inventions, this embryonic phonograph was Edison's favorite.

No doubt Sarah Josepha Hale, the mentor for thousands of women through the magazine she edited (*Godey's Lady's Book*) must have been amazed and delighted too. She had written the little story-poem to amuse her children, never expecting it to be quoted on such a notable occasion.

Through the invention of the phonograph, the voices of many famous vocalists, as well as those of statesmen, authors, and other illustrious leaders were preserved for posterity. It was a fun, pleasure-giving machine, but it also captured history on records.

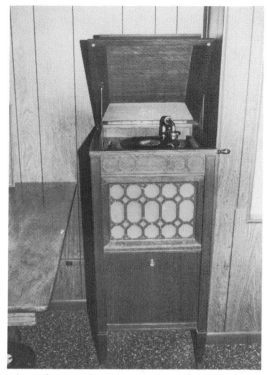

Edison phonograph, sold at Kennedy Music Co., Dixon, Illinois, patented 1916; 19″ wide, 20″ deep, 45″ high. In Illinois, **$325.**

Edison cylinder phonograph with metal horn, patented May 31, 1898; 16½″ wide, 7½″ deep, 11″ high. In Iowa, **$895.**

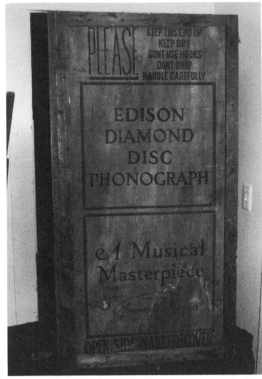

Table model Victrola with label on horn reading "flower horn;" 11½" square base, 19" diameter horn, 20" long. In Illinois, $450.

Wooden packing box for Edison Phonograph; 24" wide, 24" deep, 47" high. In Wisconsin, $100. Also seen in Illinois, $400.

Graphophone, made by the Columbia Phonograph Co. of New York, patented March 20, 1897; used the standard cylinder and the 5" cylinder by removing the cylinder holder; 15" wide, 11½" deep, 10" high. In Iowa, $1,895.

Music cabinet used to hold cylinders; 16½″ square, 33½″ high. In Illinois, $195.

Piano stool that adjusts in height; 14½″ diameter. In Illinois, $145.

Music cabinet with five shelves inside and beveled mirror at top; 18″ wide, 15″ deep, 45″ high. In Michigan, $325.

Record cabinet for 150 records, made by Pooley Furniture Co., Philadelphia, Pa., patented December 27, 1910; 28″ wide, 21″ deep, 36″ high. In Michigan, $335.

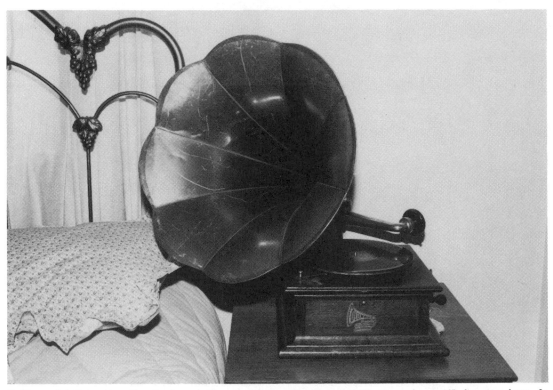

Table model Columbian Graphophone with red morning glory horn; 13½" square base, 19" diameter horn. In Colorado, $925.

In contrast to music boxes or phonographs, parlor organs required considerable skill to play. Playing the organ required musical knowledge and good coordination. The feet had to pump the pedals up and down, and the fingers, as they pressed the proper keys, had to pull out certain stops, since these buttons helped produce specific sounds. Despite such athletic and musical requirements, recitals and sings around the pump organ were a delightful form of entertainment in the late 1800s and early 1900s. Many pump organ cases were made of walnut. Oak examples are less common. Small projecting stands for kerosene lamps were frequently incorporated in the design of the organs so that the player could see both the keys and the music.

Accessory items were available for the music area. For the piano, a special stool (sometimes with claw and ball feet) might accommodate the player. The seat on round types could be twirled up or down to adjust to the height of the sitter.

Cabinets were designed to hold various necessities, such as disks, tune sheets, music rolls, or songbooks and sheet music. Except when some child was told to practice when he'd rather be playing ball, not a piano, the music area was a social center where good fellowship was enjoyed. The golden oak parlor was a pleasant place to be.

56

Windsor organ; 43¹/₂" wide, 24" deep, 75" high. In Iowa, **$1,190.**

5   Dinner Time!

Generous sized tables were a must in dining rooms a few generations ago, since large families were the norm. When the children reached adulthood and married, the ancestral tree bulged with fledglings. If everyone came bursting home for the holidays, an extension table with its many leaves could be labeled essential. Casual, paper plate entertaining was unheard of. When someone was invited for Sunday dinner, the best china (and manners too) came out. Even in a home of moderate means, the groaning table was a colorful shimmer of quivering homemade jellies, home-canned beet pickles, snappy crisp green pickles, freshly baked bread, fluffy potatoes, buttery vegetables, and succulent meats. Such a meal would be scandalously incomplete without several fruit-filled pies for dessert.

There were bone dishes, individual salt dips, butter pats, celery vases for whole stalks with leafy ends, and caster sets for vinegars and oils. With a plate for everything and everything in its place, a table, of necessity, had to grow in size to accommodate the people, the settings, and all that food.

Down on the farm, there were the threshers. Groups of neighbors took turns going from farm to farm as all worked together to gather the harvest. On the assigned day, the men with their teams of horses and wagons arrived early in the morning to go out into the fields, where they pitched up the cut stalks. A man on the wagon forked and stacked them neatly between the high end posts. When full, the wagon swayed away into the yard, where a smoke-belching threshing machine gobbled up the stalks and spewed forth the separated grain. The wives and daughters of the farmers helped the hostess-housewife prepare a generous noon meal with thickly sliced tomatoes and corn on the cob dripping with freshly churned butter. Home raised, crisply fried chicken was sure to be a part of the late summer menu. The children and women ate after the men had their fill. The kitchen might be bake-oven hot, but despite this, the women enjoyed chatting together as they cleared away the dishes, washed them in suds-filled dishpans, rinsed them with hot water poured from the teakettle heating on the range (stove), and wiped them dry with feedsack towels.

Extension table with one 15" leaf, center support pillar and paw feet; 48" diameter, 30" high. In Michigan, **$1,450.**

Unless there was a pump in the kitchen, water had to be hauled in from the well. The children helped carry it in to meet the cooking and cleaning requirements. A farm windmill might pump water from deep in the ground to fill the huge metal trough so the horses could drink.

After sprawling on the porch or under the trees for a brief rest, the men resumed their labors in the hot fields. The neighbors, separated by miles of country roads, looked forward to this time of being together. The work was hot and hard (no air conditioning or plumbing), whether in the kitchen or in the field, but there was a friendship in sharing labor. The children, when not assigned tasks, had an opportunity to play together. This cooperative era has slipped off into history, but "old threshers' reunions" are held to recall the time when that big monster was a part of summer. Indeed, big oak extension tables are also a part of this heritage.

Extension table with center supporting leg; 42" square, 28" high with four leaves, each 12" wide. In Wisconsin, **$850.**

Extension table with center-leg support and two 10" leaves; 42" square, 30" high. In Iowa, **$525.**

Extension table with two center support legs; 46" square, 29½" high; six 12"-wide leaves enable the table to extend to 117". In Wisconsin, $895.

Extension table supported by base with four carved lions' heads; 48" × 56" × 31" high. In Iowa, $2,750.

Extension table with pedestal base, legs that pull out to extend table and three 11" leaves; 48" diameter, 30" high. In Michigan, $950.

Close-up of lion's head with paw feet that serve as supports for extension table.

Extension table with center supporting leg; 42" square, 28½" high, four leaves, each 12" wide. In Iowa, $525. Set of four cane bottom chairs, $550.

Extension table with center leg support; 42" square, 30" high. In Iowa, **$550.**

Tables to accommodate crowds could be square with heavy legs or of a round pedestal variety. Literature from the library at Grand Rapids, Michigan, states that a pillar extension table was put on the market by Stowe and Davis in 1887. The early examples were constructed from plain-sawed oak, but when the demand for them increased, they were offered in quarter-sawed oak, walnut, and mahogany. They wholesaled at a low, low fifty to seventy-five cents a running foot. The price was probably double at retail stores. They were available in various sizes from six feet, when extended, to twelve feet.

Dropleaf tables that might or might not be expandable were referred to as kitchen tables. A squared, turned leg was in style in the 1850s. Such tables provided a handy spot for serving the morning repast, and were sometimes called breakfast tables, especially when they had no provision for enlarging.

Pedestal dining table; 42" diameter, 30½" high. In Iowa, **$550.** *Set of four mission chairs,* **$210.**

*Three examples of pedestal bases for extension tables. In Iowa, **$1,295** for middle example.*

*Dinette table with splayed legs—30" square, 30" high; cane seat, splatback chairs—38" high. In Iowa, table **$440;** chairs **$195** each.*

Close-up of cane seat chair from dinette set.

Dropleaf extension table, 42" × 26", with one drop leaf in down position; 30" high. In Illinois, **$250.**

Literally hundreds of thousands of small, cane-bottom side chairs were manufactured during the Victorian era in the mid- to late-1800s. Generally they were made of walnut, not of light hued oak as these two examples are.

In the golden period, dining room chairs (or diners as they were often called) had designs pressed into the backs. Seats could be wooden or formed from cane. Factories in Grand Rapids and other places loaded seatless chairs on wagons and delivered them to certain homes. Housewives, hired on a piecework basis and, perhaps, aided by children, wove the cane through the adjacent holes drilled in the seat frames at the factory.

Cane seat side chair with demi arms has a Victorian influence; 34" high. In Wisconsin, **$125** *each in a set of four.*

Cane seat side chair with concave front rung and finger hold on top rail; Victorian influence; 33" high. In Illinois, **$125** *each in a set of four.*

Cane seat pressed-back chair; 40" high. In Colorado, **$125.**

Cane seat chair with pressed-back floral design; 41" high. In Ohio, **$140.**

Cane seat pressed-back chair, 39" high. In Michigan, **$110.**

Cane seat pressed-back chair with stick and ball design above back rail and below seat at front; 40" high. In Illinois, **$155.**

Cane seat pressed-back chair; 41" high. In Illinois, $125.

Cane seat pressed-back chair; 35½" high. In Illinois, $125.

Cane seat pressed-back chair with arrow back slats; 44" high. In Iowa, $825 for a set of four.

Cane seat double-pressed-back chair, 41" high. In Michigan, $535 for a set of four.

When a groove surrounded the empty center of the seat, the ends of water-soaked, prewoven sheets of cane cut slightly larger than the vacant space were pushed into the grooves. After it was stretched taut and straight, glue and a strip of spline just large enough to fit into the groove held the "pressed cane" in place.

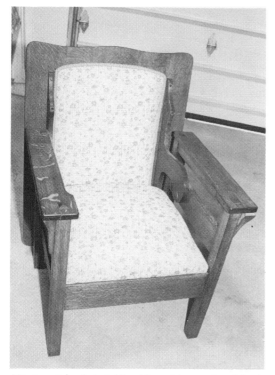

Mission-style chair table with cushion seat and back. See following picture for table position. In Illinois, **$495.**

Mission-style chair table in table position; 27" wide, 35" deep, 30" high. In Illinois, **$495.**

Brass plates, cut in decorative patterns, were used to enhance furniture, including the backs of "diners." The furniture designer, David W. Kendall, who was hired by the Grand Rapids Phoenix Furniture Company in 1879, introduced the use of trims other than wooden carvings. Metallic ornamentations were one of his innovations. Naturally, other firms were quick to copy his successful ideas.

Chair seats could be of solid wood or have a leather-type seat. At times a back would be veneered. As can be seen, chairs were produced in a variety of styles. Plainer, less expensive versions were customarily assigned to kitchen duty.

Storage units for dishes, table linens, and silver were handy in the dining room. One dating from the last quarter of the nineteenth century demonstrates that Victorian craftsmen in factories enjoyed creating decorated furniture. The hanging bunches of fruit in the sunken molded panels and the other applied carvings are well executed, as is the fretwork on the top above the marble. Most of these were made of walnut, but examples in ash were offered by some manufacturers since the common use of that wood dates from the 1850s or 1860s.

The terms sideboard and buffet are used interchangeably by different sources. The selected name in this book is sideboard, except when the piece possesses a glassed-in portion for display purposes. Such pieces will be referred to as china buffets. While both buffet and sideboard are correct nomenclature, it is more consistent to choose one descriptive word.

Columns, applied carvings, roundels (circular decorations such as a medallion), ornamental handles, unusual fronts including serpentine (snakelike curves), projection tops (hanging out over the bottom surface), rolled drawers, and paw or Empire-type scroll feet added decorative dimension to sideboards.

Grotesques is the name given to unusual, unnatural forms of either whole or partial humans or animals mixed with flowers, foliage, and fruits to create bizarre ornaments. Grotesques can be seen on the illustrated sideboard.

Cane seat pressed-back chair, 41" high. In Iowa, $446 for a set of four.

Side chair with simulated leather seat; 39½" high. In Colorado, $85 each in a set of two.

*1920-era dinette extension table—48" × 36", 30" high; two chairs, 34" high. In Illinois, table **$175**; pair of chairs **$50**.*

*Cane seat chair with veneer back and heart-shaped finger hold; 37" high. In Illinois, **$110** each in a set of four.*

*Marble-top sideboard with circa 1860 Victorian influence; 48" wide, 22" deep, 79½" high. In South Carolina, **$1,575**.*

Sideboard with swell-front top drawers, serpentine middle doors, and paw feet; 49" wide, 23" deep, 56" high. In Michigan, **$380.**

Sideboard with serpentine drawers and applied decorations; 44" wide, 22" deep, 75" high. In Illinois, **$1,250.**

Sideboard with swell-front center drawers, pressed designs on side doors and cabriole legs; 66" wide, 24" deep, 64" high. In Iowa, **$1,395.**

Sideboard with applied decorations on crest and doors; 42″ wide, 20″ deep, 72½″ high. In Connecticut, $750.

Sideboard with serpentine projection front drawers; 42″ wide, 21″ deep, 79¼″ high. In Georgia, $650.

Sideboard; 41″ wide, 18″ deep, 56″ high. In South Carolina, $525.

Sideboard with applied decorations; 52″ wide, 23″ deep, 76″ high. In Maryland, $795.

71

*China buffet with two convex glass china closets flanking central storage area; 62" wide, 21" deep, 70" high. In Illinois, **$1,595.***

When you cross a sideboard with a china cabinet, what do you beget? A china buffet, that's what! This is an all-inclusive term for these uncommon items. The Sears 1897 replica catalog shows and labels such a double-duty piece as a buffet. Space where table linens could be stored and plush-lined silverware drawers were present. Glass-enclosed showcases revealed hand-painted china and dainty glass treasures. At times a mirror was incorporated into the design. Styles differed greatly. The china cabinet portion could be in the belly of the buffet, or stand off to the side. A symmetrical form had two glass-protected shelf sections, one on either side of the base. Today these pieces are not easy to find, and china buffets are considered choice.

In the early decades of the 1900s, hand painting on imported "blanks" (plain china reserved for this purpose) was a popular pastime. Potteries usually backstamped this undecorated china. It is not unusual to find china made by Haviland or another recognized manufacturer that was hand-decorated by an amateur. Instructions in china painting were available through classes or from articles in ladies' magazines.

*China buffet with leaded glass and serpentine center drawer and doors; 54" wide, 20" deep, 40½" high, 11½" back rail. In Illinois, **$825.***

Clubs provided a fun way for young ladies to acquire a collection of colorful china. A member who celebrated a birthday received an inexpensive gift, such as a dessert plate or a cup and saucer, from each lady in the group. The patterns did not have to match, so an attractive assortment resulted.

One woman who now enjoys her mother's fancy dishes likes to recall that when her father, who owned a furniture store, traveled out of town, he would return with a special present of china or glass for his wife. These also could be individual pieces that did not compose a set. Such mixing created colorful displays, and variety was actually preferred.

China buffet with applied decorations; 42" wide, 19" deep, 58" high. In Iowa, **$895.**

China buffet with leaded glass in top door panel and convex glass doors; 49" wide, 20" deep, 64" high. In Michigan, **$895.**

China buffet with applied decorations on drawers and leaded glass on doors; 54" wide, 22" deep, 64" high. In Illinois, **$1,550.**

China buffet with serpentine doors and drawers; 53" wide, 22" deep, 71½" high. In Illinois, **$1,595.**

Server with swell drawer front, cabriole legs, paw feet and applied decoration on mirror top; 42" wide, 19" deep, 55" high. In Illinois, **$565.**

Sideboard with beveled mirror and applied decorations; 54" wide, 25" deep, 59" high. In Michigan, $795.

Server with swell top drawer and shelves for storage at each side; 48" wide, 18" deep, 41" high. In Iowa, $350.

Server with swell front and lamp or candle stands at each side of rear mirror; 42" wide, 21" deep, 53" high. In Illinois, $325.

China cabinet with S-curved door and side glass, paw feet, and two intricately carved figures of women, called caryatides, *holding up top shelf; 48" wide, 17" deep, 78" high. In Iowa,* **$5,500.**

Special units to display tableware were called china cabinets or closets. Although they were made with either curved glass or flat, the convex type (curves out) received a high rating. Old ones are eagerly sought and pressed into service currently. Demand is so high, new china cabinets in this style are being produced by a number of companies.

A most unusual china cabinet is pictured. It has serpentine glass (curves like a snake) on the sides as well as in the door. The top shelf is supported by two columns that are wooden carvings of women. This is an adaptation of an early Greek architectural design where depictions of human figures formed supporting pillars. The sex depicted determines what they are called. Female versions are caryatides, while male figures are atlantes.

Close-up of caryatid—the name applies to a female head used as a supporting column. If the head is male, it is called an atlantes.

China cabinet with applied wooden grill work on glass; 41" wide, 16¼" deep, 63½" high. In Pennsylvania, **$825.**

China cabinet with convex glass on door and side panels; 42" wide, 16" deep, 62½" high, 2" rail. In Iowa, $850.

China cabinet and storage unit that was once a built-in unit; 70" wide, 21" deep, 92" high. In Iowa, $2,395.

China cabinet with convex glass side panels and paw feet; 40" wide, 14" deep, 60" high. In Michigan, $975.

China cabinet with convex door and side panels, applied grotesques above pillars; 34" wide, 12" deep, 62" high. In Virginia, $695.

Corner china cabinet with concave glass door and straight glass side panels; 40½" wide, 24" deep, 69½" high. In Illinois, $1,295.

Feet too had different features with paws, glass balls seized by claws, or scroll feet being the most prevalent styles. Most glass surfaces were advertised as "double thick." This increased their ability to survive unbroken while preserving their visibility feature.

Oak corner china cabinets rate a rare ranking, and their pricetags confirm this fact. Glass in some front doors curves inward (concave).

After the dark furniture and draperies and the heavy use of bric-a-brac, many women must have welcomed the lighter colored furniture. Undoubtedly, fashion conscious housewives of the late 1800s and early 1900s embraced golden finishes greedily and gratefully.

Corner china cabinet with two convex door panels; 37" wide, 21" deep, 66½" high, 3½" rail. In Wisconsin, $1,295.

Corner china cabinet with concave door panel and applied decorations above glass panels; 36" wide, 23" deep, 72" high. In Indiana, **$1,495.**

Corner china cabinet with convex door panel; 29" wide, 17" deep, 63" high, 7½" rail. In Illinois, **$975.**

Corner china cabinet with convex door panel; 32" wide, 20" deep, 58½" high. In Pennsylvania, **$950.**

6 The Multipurpose Kitchen

Have you ever passed a bakery early in the morning and smelled bread baking? Ahhhh — what an alluring aroma! Occasionally, today's housewives mix the flour-yeast combination, knead the dough, permit it to double, and put loaves into their ovens. Soon that "homemade" smell wafts tantalizingly through the air. It is also possible to cheat a bit and buy frozen loaves to bake at home to create that special odor that lingers so delightfully.

Back in the days before instant foods, the kitchen was the center of much activity. Perhaps it was partly because Mama spent so many hours there, and the family gravitated around her. In a rural Quaker home of the 1920s (before radio's prominence and television's invention), a mother taught her two daughters poetry. There were contests to see who could recite the most lines as they shared meal tasks or worked together canning the garden's excess vegetables and fruits for winter use. As they captured red tomatoes or green beans or yellow peaches in glass jars, the summer days didn't seem so unbearably hot, despite the steaming boiler loaded with canning jars. Water at a prolonged rolling boil temperature was required to kill bacteria, but Mama and the girls enjoyed being together in spite of the steam heat.

In a musical Catholic home of that period, the fellows played guitars in the kitchen after dinner, singing along as their sisters harmonized with them. The music made the sink work seem less tedious as the girls washed, rinsed, wiped, and put away a mountain of dinner dishes. In both families, the arts helped arduous tasks seem pleasant.

Amid all this activity stood the kitchen aids. In the 1890s, a baker's table might be present. It had a flat work surface with pullout slicing boards, drawers for storing cutlery, and perhaps two bins. One was large enough to hold the family flour supply (say fifty pounds), while the other was divided so that possibly rye might be kept on one side and cornmeal on the other. Or, sugar could be stored in one unit, depending on the preference of the housewife. Later, someone must have decided that there was a great deal of space going to waste, so a top for spices, pots, pans, dishes, or what-

have-you was added. The table thus expanded into a baker's cabinet. Other types of storage units seem to have descended from this utilitarian piece.

Baker's cabinet; 42" wide, 28½" deep at the base, 11" deep at top section, 63" high. In Illinois, **$795.**

For example, what resembles a desk but helps feed a family? A breadboard, naturally. Notice the rolltop on the example pictured. When it is down, the unit takes on the appearance of a desk. A slide pulls out for chopping or slicing chores, and there are two bins tucked behind the doors in the base. Above is a storage area. Incised carvings add attractive designs.

Since Indiana is called the Hoosier State, it is only natural that a manufacturer would choose to name his kitchen cabinet, manufactured at New Castle, a Hoosier cabinet. This cabinet also evolved from the baker's table but offered so much more that advertisers waxed enthusiastically about its attractions. Any housewife was supposed to be overjoyed and cry out in delightful surprise when she received a gift of a stepsaving Hoosier cabinet. How could she ever desire jewelry, a new outfit, a watch, or other mundane articles when she could have a Hoosier instead? Such cabinets did lighten kitchen drudgery. They had sanitary moistureproof coffee and tea containers and cookbook, bill, coin, menu card, or recipe file holders. Cooking time charts with weights and measures were included. A metal-lined bread drawer contained holes for ventilation. Flour sifters were frequently present along with swing-out sugar jars. The durable, washable porcelain top could be pulled out to provide additional work space. A Hoosier eclipsed all possible presents. The use of this name spread until it became the generic (group) title for all cupboards of this type brought out in the early decades of the 1900s.

The Sellers Company of Elwood, Indiana, romantically christened one of their models the "June Bride." Another version was so helpful it must have been able to replace the hired girl because it was called the "Kitchen Maid." Other Indiana producers of Hoosier cabinets were Ingram Richardson Manufacturing Company, Frankfort; Wasmuth Endicott Company of Andrews; plus the Boone and Greencastle cabinets. Look for company names on brass tags, metal handles, or instruction cards and preserve them.

Breadboard resembles desk, but raised rolltop reveals pull-out breadboard; 32½" wide, 21" deep, 60" high. In Iowa, **$1,250.**

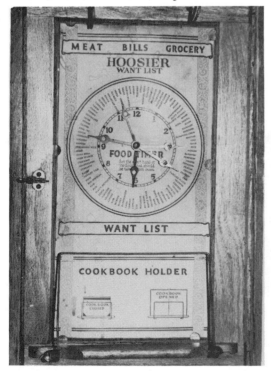

Sign found inside Hoosier cabinet.

Hoosier cabinet; 41" wide, 26½" deep, 71" high. In Iowa, **$795.**

*Sellers cabinet; 47½" wide, 26½" deep, 81¼" high. In Iowa, **$950.***

How did a family get the money for all this convenience? Fortunately, the time payment plan had been introduced. With credit, it was possible to go into debt one day and meet the purchase price gradually over extended tomorrows. For five dollars down, five dollars monthly, and a "small" interest fee, the cabinet could be "in your home working for you as you pay for it." The advertisements urged buyers, "Don't wait. Order today."

A model might include a slatted, flexible shutter or door that could be opened sideways (horizontally) or with an up or down pull (vertically). Flexible doors were made of thin strips of wood glued to a duck or linen backing. Such closures, which operated in grooves, were called tambours. A similar arrangement is found on rolltop desks. Occasionally slag glass or amber panels added color to solid doors. Hoosiers were available with an oak finish or painted with white or gray enamel. That thorough factory application of color clings as tenaciously to the wood as a miser to his money. When moderns adopt Hoosiers, they find it is disgustingly difficult to remove the paint down to the original wood.

Although catalogs offered less expensive and plainer chairs for kitchens, almost any simple kind from the dining room could be used there. This is true of tables, also. Some, with the addition of leaves, could be extended to six or twelve feet in length. Dropleaf types that did not expand were frequently mentioned in advertising as being handy for breakfast. They were offered with either oval or rectangular lines.

*Kitchen cabinet with cylinder front that covers a pull-out doughboard; 33" wide, 21" deep, 64" high. In Illinois, **$1,000.***

Sellers cabinet; 40" wide, 28" deep, 70" high. In Iowa, **$695.**

Sellers cabinet; 40½" wide, 27" deep, 70" high. In Illinois, **$595.**

Hoosier-type kitchen cabinet made in Andrews, Indiana, by the Wasmuth Endicott Co.; 40" wide, 29" deep, 71¼" high. In Iowa, **$695.**

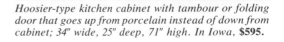

Hoosier-type kitchen cabinet with tambour or folding door that goes up from porcelain instead of down from cabinet; 34" wide, 25" deep, 71" high. In Iowa, **$595.**

*Cupboard with dry sink and pull-out work area; 50″ wide, 30″ deep, 78″ high. In Michigan, **$1,950.***

Cupboard showing the pull-out work area extended.

*Boone kitchen cabinet; 37¹/₂″ wide, 23″ deep, 71¹/₄″ high. In Iowa, **$725.***

*Hoosier-type kitchen cabinet; 43″ wide, 26″ deep, 70¹/₂″ high. In Wisconsin, **$695.***

Greencastle kitchen cabinet; 42" wide, 28" deep, 67½" high. In Illinois, **$795.**

Ash kitchen desk cabinet with spoon carving on drawer and door fronts; 41" wide, 17" deep, 82" high. See next picture for view of writing area. In Illinois, **$750.**

Ash kitchen desk cabinet with drop-front writing area exposed.

Pie safe with six pierced-tin panels; 41" wide, 15" deep, 56" high. In Illinois, $495.

An unusual chair table of a late date copies the pine or poplar versions that served as spacesavers in America's early days. When the top is swung down to rest on the arms of the chair, it functions as a table. Instead of the slotted construction shown in the arms of the one photographed (on page 67), pins were used in eighteenth-century examples to keep the top anchored in place.

Oak pie safes are not common, but many were produced in walnut or poplar. The diamond-and-circle combination design shown is punched from the outside in. The little holes could be pierced from inside to the outside also. Pie safe was a good title because pastries were placed on the shelves, where they received some ventilation to retard molding, yet were protected from flies or rodents. Flies were a big problem, especially in the rural areas. Sticky flypaper or patented traps were used to catch these buzzing, biting pests. Mice could not chew through metal, so the tin sheets frustrated their efforts to reach the baked goods. Most of these safes date from the last half of the 1800s.

Kitchen cupboards could be made attractive by the use of incised or applied carvings. Many had glass enclosed doors at the top, drawers, and solid doors at the base. Ornamental cornices frequently crowned the top.

Stepback cupboard; 36½" wide, 16½" deep, 83" high. In Iowa, $795.

Stepback cupboard; 43" wide, 18" deep, 89½" high. In Iowa, $1,295.

Stepback cupboard with pie shelf; 41" wide, 17" deep, 91" high. In Iowa, $850.

Stepback cupboard with pie shelf; 38" wide, 16" deep, 80" high. In Illinois, $795.

Straight front cupboard; 36½" wide, 16½" deep, 72" high. In Illinois, $595.

Closed cupboard (without glass at top) with pie shelf; 43" wide, 16½" deep, 84" high. In Indiana, $795.

Kitchen cabinet with straight front and pressed designs on drawers and doors; 40" wide, 16" deep, 77" high. In Illinois, **$695.**

Late 1800s corner cupboard with two drawers and two doors; 40" wide, 23" deep, 78" high. In Michigan, **$1,750.**

Preserving food and keeping it fresh for use was a problem. In the cold of a northern winter, it was possible to have a window box attached to the outside of a kitchen window. Foods could be kept cold (sometimes frozen) by placing them in it. In warmer areas, fruit cellars were dug to create a little room where perishables could be stored. On the western plains where tornados were a fright, these cellars served as a haven when fierce windstorms threatened. With the family sheltered safely underground, and the wooden trapdoor fastened securely over the steps, the violent, whirling wind with its power to sweep and swirl buildings or people lost its ability to carry them off to Dorothy's Wizard in the fantastic Land of Oz. Springhouses were also conveniences in pre-electricity days. A building with thick stone or brick walls was built over a cool spring that bubbled up out of the ground or over the farmstead well. This provided cool storage for perishable foods. Wells at times functioned as a place where objects were suspended to keep them chilled.

The icebox must have seemed like a precious treasure when it was introduced. In a chest version,

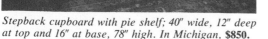

Stepback cupboard with pie shelf; 40" wide, 12" deep at top and 16" at base, 78" high. In Michigan, **$850.**

the ice and food stood side-by-side in a metal-lined wooden box. In a refrigerator, air circulated constantly, based on the principle that hot air rises. Warm air would hit the block of ice in the top, cool, and descend to the bottom. As it warmed, it rose again. The large crystal cube was placed inside a lift-top compartment at the top or behind a door in the front. As melting occurred, the water flowed through a tube and out a hole at the base into a pan provided for that purpose. It was a trick to empty this receptacle before it overflowed and necessitated a hasty mop-up.

Since distributing ice was a summer season business, many companies combined their efforts and supplied coal to customers during the cold months. How was ice delivered to city consumers? As late as the 1930s, a horse and wagon, later a truck, plied the streets, covering definite areas on specified days. Cards supplied by the company were placed in a house's front window. The cards indicated the amount of ice desired — twenty-five, fifty, seventy-five, or even one hundred pounds. The stalwart driver, with a body builder's type muscles, hopped off the seat, poked pointed tongs into a precut block, and slung the dripping pounds on his leather protected shoulder to carry it in the back door and deposit it in the box. Meanwhile, back at his vehicle, the neighborhood kids swarmed about the wagon stealing slivers of ice to suck. Invariably, the burly drivers were kindly tolerant of adventurous lads who stealthily swang up on the tailgate for a cooling tour of the neighborhood. In the early twentieth century, the cry, "The ice man's coming!" caused as much excitement as the bells of the Good Humor cart do today.

How did country people obtain ice? Through a do-it-yourself, cooperative effort. Rural rivers were not as apt to be contaminated as they are now. When streams froze in the winter, neighboring farmers banded together to cut ice. They marked off blocks and sawed along the lines to form huge cubes that they hauled away to store until summer. At times a rundown vacant house was filled with layers of ice insulated with a thick covering of sawdust or sand between the stacks. When a farmer needed ice, he picked up a block from this source. Ice picks or special shavers were used to chip small pieces of ice for cooling beverages. Sanitation was not a major consideration in those days.

Ash ice box, patented June 30, 1925, with brass plaque reading, "A Life Preserver for Food"; 21" wide, 16" deep, 48" high. In Iowa, **$445.**

Buffalo icebox; 29" wide, 19" deep, 42½" high. In Maryland, **$595.**

Icebox with Estey Royale brass plaque that is not original; 25" wide, 18" deep, 38" high. In Ohio, $475.

Lorraine icebox made in LaCrosse, Wisconsin, by LaCrosse Refrig. Corp.; 31" wide, 15" deep, 42" high. In Illinois, $495.

As a hot-time treat, ice cream was made outdoors. Rich cream from the farm cows, combined with eggs, sugar, and flavoring, was poured into a cylindrical, metal, lidded container with paddles inside. Ice pulverized in a gunnysack by repeated blows from a hammer was placed in a wooden bucket around the container. Lots of salt on the ice promoted melting to help cool the contents rapidly. Turning a crank rotated the cylinder, which thickened the cream. When the handle became hard to turn, the mixture was almost solidified. The dasher was removed and more salted ice was packed around and over the container to allow the contents to "ripen." Everyone vied for the opportunity to lick the dasher. Finally, it was ready. How shivery cold that ice cream tasted on a hot summer night.

The kitchen was a multipurpose room. Besides being a cooking, eating, canning, and preserving site, it was the place where the family laundry and personal washing were done before pipes brought water into the house. A washbowl and pitcher were handily placed on a shelf or stand for quick cleansings before meals, and a roller towel was nearby. A comb case of tin, or perhaps wood, might include a mirror. There might be a hanging cabinet to hold a man's shaving soap, brush, and sharp-edged razor, womanly toilet articles, or minor medicinal needs. Traditionally, a washtub occupied the center of the floor on Saturday night, and water heated on the stove was poured into it so that each family member could have a sit-down bath. On Monday, the housewife toted water from the well, heated it, and scrubbed the laundry in the kitchen unless she had a washroom. Afterward she hung it outside over fences or on lines to dry, winter or summer.

The kitchen was often a study and game room since the family could gather around the table there. Children could work on school projects at the kitchen table or enjoy a game. In cold months the kitchen was a social center because it was usually the warmest room in the house. No wonder an unknown poet wrote, "No matter where I seat my guests, they seem to like my kitchen best."

Octagonal cellarette (liquor cabinet) with revolving top and single front door; 17" wide, 54" high. In Alaska, $325.

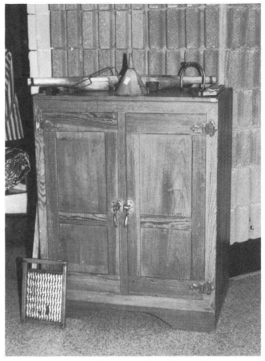

Icebox; 32" wide, 22" deep, 41" high. In Illinois, $475.

Comb case with spoon carving on front of base; 11¼" wide, 15" high. In Iowa, $110.

Medicine cabinet with towel rack, often found in the kitchen, held shaving paraphernalia as well as medicinal supplies; 18" wide, 5½" deep, 22" high. In Illinois, $165.

7　The Student's Corner

What pieces of furniture would a student's quarters or a home office or library require? Count them off — a chair, desk, bookcases, and, perhaps, a library table to hold periodicals. Of course, lighting would be given prime consideration.

A type of desk that was popular in the golden oak period was made in combination with a bookcase so that it became a versatile two-in-one unit. Most had the same basic design. The desk portion was devoted to drawers or cupboard doors and a fall-front or drop-lid writing compartment. This section might be referred to as a slant front when the drop portion angled in from the hinged bottom to the top. The desk was joined on the side by a tall, slender bookcase, frequently with a convex glass in the door, but sometimes with flat glass in the opening. This enclosure helped keep the books dust free. While most of the combos followed this pattern, the varying styles ranged from plain to fancy. There could be mirrors and shelves above the slant front, or the lids might be simply decorated or elaborately embellished with incised designs or applied carvings. The feet could be brackets, scrolls, paws, almost straight, or with slight curves.

You will realize, as you face one of these desks, that most were built with the bookshelves on the left. As a right-handed scholar removed a required book with his left hand, he could continue writing without interruption. A lefty would find it necessary to put down his pen and reach out for the volume he wanted. You might wonder if any models were made with the divisions reversed. While these left-handed desks were produced, they were never common. Those for the right-handed people predominated. A type that would accommodate either writer had a bookcase on each side of the fall front.

Combination bookcase-desk; 37" wide, 12" deep, 71" high. In Illinois, **$825.**

Combination bookcase-desk; 42" wide, 13" deep, 68½" high. In Illinois, **$795.**

Combination bookcase-desk; 37" wide, 13" deep, 76" high. In Iowa, $895.

Combination bookcase-desk with "open book" appearance of drop lid, and drawer above writing area; 42½" wide, 13" deep, 67½" high. In Iowa, $825.

Combination bookcase-desk with unusual convex-glass-enclosed storage compartment above writing area; 41½" wide, 13½" deep, 68" high. In Iowa, $1,195.

Combination bookcase-desk with convex bookcase door, leaded glass above drop front, applied decoration on top rail and paw feet; 42" wide, 14" deep, 76" high. In Iowa, $1,750.

Combination bookcase-desk; 37" wide, 14" deep, 72" high. In Wisconsin, $795.

Combination bookcase-desk with flat-glass door front and applied decorations; 38" wide, 14" deep, 74" high. In Iowa, $1,095.

Combination bookcase-desk with desk on left-hand side to accommodate a left-handed writer (the majority of combination desks have the desk section on the right-hand side); 43" wide, 14" deep, 72" high. In Illinois, $995.

Another with ambidextrous traits had its glass-enclosed space for books under the fall front. One Wisconsin version is referred to as a Sheboygan desk. A mirror between two small, rounded out drawers appears to be supported by two winged creatures with animal bodies and fish tails. As previously mentioned, these figures are called grotesques. A simpler look was achieved when the bookcase featured open shelves.

Combination bookcase-desk with desk on the left-hand side to accommodate a left-handed writer; 41½" wide, 13½" deep, 72" high. In Illinois, $1,425.

Combination bookcase-desk from the P. T. Barnum estate; 55½" wide, 15" deep, 78½" high. In Colorado, $2,250.

Sheboygan desk with grotesques flanking mirror; 31½" wide, 13½" deep, 72" high. In Wisconsin, $1,295.

Close-up of grotesque that serves as mirror support on Sheboygan desk.

Combination Mission-style bookcase-desk with fall-front desk in center; 63" wide, 17" deep, 51" high. In Michigan, $750.

Fall-front parlor desk; 27" wide, 14" deep, 42" high. In Iowa, $395.

More often, fall-front desks had a writing area with a drawer and stood on high legs so that the sitter had ample knee space. Lids and back galleries were usually ornamented. This type was advertised as a parlor style.

Combination stacking bookcase-desk, called "The Herkiner," made by F. E. Hale Mfg. Co., Herkiner, N.Y.; 34" wide, 14" deep, 59" high. In Michigan, $950.

Combination bookcase-desk made in six sections; 34" wide, 12" deep, 60" high. In Illinois, $795.

Fall-front parlor desk with applied decorations, mirror and provisions for books below; 30" wide, 12" deep, 62" high. In Iowa, $625.

Fall-front parlor desk; 27" wide, 13" deep, 64" high. In Michigan, $595.

97

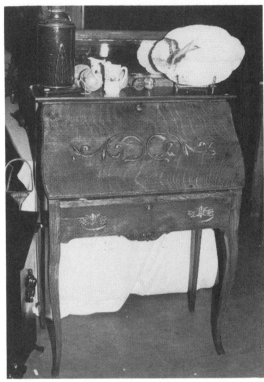

Fall-front parlor desk; 29½" wide, 15" deep, 50" high. In Illinois, $395.

Fall-front desk; 33" wide, 12" deep, 62" high. In Illinois, $795.

Fall-front parlor desk; 27½" wide, 14" deep, 42" high. In Iowa, $495.

Fall-front parlor desk, back is finished to resemble front with a fake fall front and drawer; 26½" wide, 16½" deep, 52½" high. In Iowa, $825.

Fall-front table desk resembles the walnut Victorian style circa 1860; 36" wide, 24" deep, 58" high. In Pennsylvania, $795.

Fall-front parlor desk with incised and applied decorations and mirror on back rail; 29" wide, 14" deep, 58" high. In Iowa, $725.

Tabletop drop-lid desks with incised lines and turned legs were common in the late 1800s. Walnut prevailed but light wood versions were made. Another Victorian type was a fall front on top of what appears to be a low chest of drawers. The incised parallel lines and brass pulls date it to the late 1800s when Eastlake styles were imitated.

Fall-front desk with bureau base; 31" wide, 16" deep, 46" high. In Iowa, $675.

Fall-front secretary; 30" wide, 16" deep, 84" high. In Wisconsin, **$1,350.**

Secretaries are tall units consisting of a desk with drawers beneath the writing surface and a tall bookcase on top. These were a holdover from the Victorian era.

Fall-front secretary; 32" wide, 18" deep, 81" high. In Illinois, **$1,295.**

Fall-front secretary; 36" wide, 16" deep, 86" high. In Iowa, **$1,495.**

Fall-front secretary; 42" wide, 19" deep, 82" high. In Wisconsin, **$1,995.**

Around 1872, the Phoenix Furniture Company of Grand Rapids, Michigan, manufactured a "French cylinder" desk described as "unique." A sliding lid closed down over the writing surface and pigeonholes. One key locked all seventeen drawers at once. At first, black walnut was the chosen wood. A golden oak period secretary is pictured that features a cylinder top over a series of drawers and a cupboard base.

Rolltop desks are as popular today as they were when their golden finish was new. When the desk is being used, the fabric-lined, flexible, parallel slats slide back in grooves. If there is clutter on the writing area, it is a simple matter to pull the rolltop down to hide the debris. A youth size is larger than a child's but too small to serve most adults.

When the roll has a double ripple in it, it is referred to as an S-curve. The C version rounds out only once.

Cylinder front secretary; 38" wide, 22" deep, 90½" high. In Iowa, **$2,295.**

Student-size rolltop desk; 36¼" wide, 22" deep, 37" high. In Illinois, **$425.**

S-curve rolltop desk; 53½" wide, 23½" deep, 46" high. In Illinois, **$1,500.**

Rolltop desk; 60" wide, 34" deep, 42½" high. In Illinois, **$1,550.**

Folding furniture is convenient when space is limited or when portability is important. A desk that folds is one example, as is the bookcase pictured.

Office chairs of the golden time could be of generous size. Many had special features. Some tilted. Others could be twirled around and around for height adjustment. Most afforded a degree of comfort to the user, and those with designs pressed into the back slats were not uncommon.

Bookcases were and are always needed. Many were quite plain while others were incised or had carvings applied to their surfaces. Open lattice-work could prove attractive.

Rolltop desk; 40" wide, 25" deep, 41" high. In Wisconsin, **$1,450.**

Folding bookshelf; 24" wide, 8" deep, 44" high. In Colorado, **$195.**

Folding lady's desk; 32" wide, 17½" deep, 26½" high. In Illinois, **$275.**

Swivel office chair; 23" arm to arm, 38" high. In Iowa, **$360.**

Swivel desk chair; 23" arm to arm, 35" high. In Iowa, **$145.**

Bookcase; 38½" wide, 13" deep, 53" high. In Iowa, **$675.**

Bookcase with paw feet; 40" wide, 13" deep, 59" high. In Illinois, **$825.**

Bookcase with lattice work on top door panels and applied decorations; 39" wide, 12½" deep, 72" high. In Iowa, **$1,495.**

Bookcase; 39" wide, 11½" deep, 57½" high. In Wisconsin, **$495.**

A breakfront case is one where the center vertical section juts out from the sections on each side.

Bookcase with three doors and four front paw feet; 55" wide, 14" deep, 60" high. In Wisconsin, **$1,025.**

Bookcase; 40" wide, 14" deep, 76" high. In Illinois, **$595.**

Bookcase with applied decoration on back rail; 36" wide, 13" deep, 66" high. In Illinois, **$695.**

Bookcase with three doors and paw feet; 55¼" wide, 14" deep, 67½" high. In Indiana, **$1,500.**

China cabinet with three front legs and applied decorations on stiles; 40" wide, 18" deep, 57" high. In Michigan, **$750.**

A common type bookcase of the golden oak period was composed of individual units that could be stacked together. The top was one piece and the apron and legs were a component. In between, various rectangular sections could be placed as desired. These were enclosed with glass doors that pulled up and slid in at the top. Fumed or antique finishes also could be chosen. When leaded glass was incorporated, it made the pieces quite distinctive.

Bookcase in five sections with three doors that pull up and slide in; 34" wide, 11" deep, 50" high. In Iowa, $595.

Bookcase in six sections with four leaded glass doors that pull up and slide in; 35¹/₂" wide, 14" deep, 65" high. In Iowa, $825.

Bookcase in six sections with four glass doors that pull up and slide in; 34" wide, 11" deep, 59" high. In Iowa, $750.

Library tables to hold books, periodicals, and newspapers were available in a variety of styles. Many homes were not large enough to have a special room as a study. In such cases, desks and bookcases could be assigned space in the bedroom or parlor. Usually the library table graced the living room so that literature was readily at hand when someone plopped down in a comfortable chair to read. The new, side-by-side, desk-bookcase combination was one of the welcomed additions to homes with the golden touch decor.

Bookcase with leaded glass at the top of the flat glass doors and paw feet; 61" wide, 12" deep, 63" high. In Iowa, **$1,125.**

Library table with pressed design on drawer and apron and base shelf; 36" wide, 23" deep, 29" high. In Iowa, **$345.**

Library table with one drawer at each end and scroll feet; 42" wide, 28" deep, 30" high. In Michigan, **$225.**

Mission-style library table with one drawer; 48" wide, 30" deep, 30" high. In Alaska, **$725.**

8   Childhood Treasures

Doll bed with pressed design in head- and footboards; 12½" wide, 24½" long, 15" high at headboard, 9¼" high at footboard. In Wisconsin, **$125.**

Child's ash doll dresser; 13½" wide, 7" deep, 26½" high. In Wisconsin, **$185.**

"Oh, isn't this darling! It's so petite and not expensive," a tall man squealed in imitation of his wife as he minced his way through an antiques display. In his normal masculine voice, he continued with a chuckle, "I examine furniture but my wife chooses these little bitties she calls cute or cunning."

Dainty articles can excite the antiques taste buds of many ladies and help them recall nostalgic childhood memories. Maybe that's partly why dealing in dolls is lucrative business currently. Grown-ups also enjoy searching for the proper pint-sized furniture to complement their collections. A little collapsible doll bed with pressed designs on the head and foot boards could hold a sleepy pretend baby. An old fashioned ticking, the original mattress, covers the slats.

Adults can capture children's items to give them pleasure, but turnabout's fair play. Children also have models from the adult world sized especially for them. A small version of a dresser, emulating its larger counterparts, might have an oak appearance but actually could be ash. The mirror on the example shown is interesting because of the imitation bamboo frame around it.

The name chiffonier (also spelled with two n's) has a French derivation. A chiffonier is a narrow, tall chest of drawers that may or may not include a mirror. Children's sizes were copies of those that housed Mama's and Papa's union suits or other undergarments modestly hidden from sight.

A child's cupboard could hold treasures or toys. A small plant or lamp stand in wee dimensions could have served youngsters from past generations.

Child's doll dresser; 14" wide, 7" deep, 14¼" high. In Iowa, **$225.**

Child's doll dresser; 12½" wide, 6½" deep, 11" high. In Illinois, **$145.**

Child's chiffonier with swing mirror; 22" wide, 13" deep, 30" to chiffonier top, 16½" high mirror. In Illinois, **$600.**

Child's chiffonier with swing mirror; 22" wide, 13" deep, 30" to chiffonier top, 16½" high mirror. In Iowa, **$695.**

Child's doll cupboard; 7½" wide, 4" deep, 9½" high, 1½" back rail. In Illinois, **$125.**

Child's plant stand; 11½" square, 19½" high. In Illinois, **$125.**

Child's plank seat rocker; 29" high. In Illinois, **$165.**

Rockers or other chairs resembled mongrel puppies because they frequently possessed mixed breeds of wood in their structure. Some species were soft enough to shape into seats. Others turned well to form spindles, while others could be bent with ease. Notice the bent arms on the rocker illustrated.

A pressed back, cane seat, spindles with a ropelike twist, and bent arms characterize this chair.

A straight slat look cries "Mission!" This stoic, stocky style with its angular lines was in vogue early in the 1900s. Naturally there were examples available for the small-size set, as the chair and rocker on page 113 exemplify. For more on mission furniture, turn to Chapter 12.

A fascinating variety of highchairs have been made. Some could be purchased with or without a drop table (tray) that could be swung into position after the child was seated and help keep him in place. Some highchairs have bow backs. With its machine-made and skimpy number of spindles, the one pictured is distantly related to and is a debased form of the graceful, multispindled, handcrafted Windsor chairs that were popular in this country in the late 1700s.

Child's cane seat pressed-back rocker with twisted spindles; 15½" arm to arm, 28" high. **$245.**

Child's mission-style chair; 29" high. In Illinois, **$110.**

Child's mission-style rocker; 17½" arm to arm, 28" high. In Iowa, **$165.**

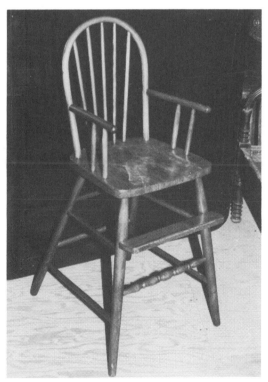

Bow-back youth chair; 14" arm to arm. 38" high. In Iowa, **$155.**

Veneer-back youth chair; 14" arm to arm, 40" high. In Iowa, **$165.**

A thin slice of veneer with an attractive pattern could be glued to a shaped back to add to its attractive qualities.

Frequently "seasoned hardwoods" was the term that described furniture construction in vintage catalogs. "Rock elm" yielded a sturdy sound. This chair is an example of construction using a mixture of maple and oak.

Quite often chairs were offered in a choice of solid wooden seats or cane. Buyers could select the chair bottom they preferred.

Highchair with table or tray; 40½" high. In Ohio, **$195.**

Pressed-back highchair with table or tray; 40½" high. In Iowa, **$225.**

Pressed-back highchair with cane seat and table or tray; 43½" high. In Illinois, **$315.**

Cane seat youth chair with pressed/carved-back flamingo decoration; 42" high. In Iowa, **$240.**

With its bright pink or red feathers that remind one of flames, it is no wonder that a long-legged, tropical wading bird was named a flamingo. A design of this creature with its sweeping, curved neck is pressed into the back of a child's highchair that does not have a "table." This youth chair for the older child could be pulled up to the table at mealtime. Chiseling or cutting was often used to add a deeper touch to a pressed decoration. The flamingo design is intricately executed. Contrast it with the pressed pattern on the rail of the next highchair and you will note a great variance in the depth of the design.

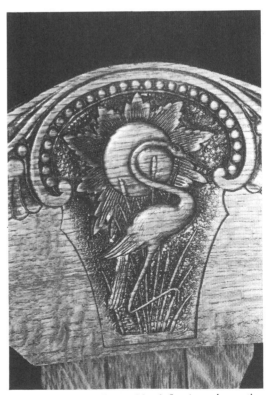

Close-up of pressed/carved-back flamingo decoration on youth chair.

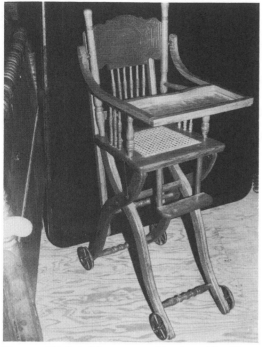

Cane seat highchair/go-cart combination with table or tray; 40" high. In Iowa, $395.

Cane seat highchair/go-cart combination with table or tray and pressed pineapple slats; 40" high. In Iowa, $450.

Infants were riding around in their own special convertibles long before automobile manufacturers designed cars of that name to please sporty adults. Ads assured buyers that a push of a button would adjust special highchairs, converting them into go-carts. This gave a wee one his own wheels. The modern slogan, "You've come a long way, Baby," instantly comes to mind.

This example is a variation from the ordinary convertible. It is a combination highchair and go-cart with a cane back and seat. Three positions could include a rocker.

Desks were available in child size, and curtain (now called roll) tops in miniature were popular. As mentioned, when the roll takes a double sweep, it is called an S-curve.

Cane seat and back highchair/go-cart combination with table or tray missing; in down position, 13½" wide, 16½" deep, 24" high. In Illinois, $225.

116

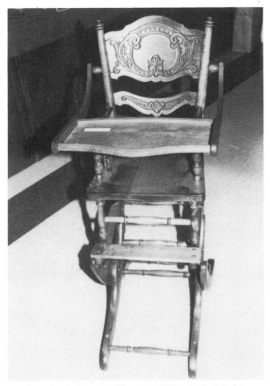

Rocking highchair; 17¼" wide, 40" high. In Michigan, **$425.**

Rocking highchair shown in down or rocking position.

Child's lift-lid desk; 27" wide, 18" deep, 35" high. In Iowa, **$336.**

Child's combination bookcase-desk with desk on left-hand side to accommodate left-hand writer; 38" wide, 11" deep, 47" high. In Iowa, **$650.**

117

It is interesting that most adult-sized bookcase-desks have the drop-lid desk section on the right as one faces it. Apparently this would leave a writer's left hand free to reach for a book when needed. If the desk is on the other side, it probably served a left-handed person. Curiously, the children's pieces illustrated both have the desk at the left.

Apparently parents sought up-to-date furniture for their offsprings, and replicas of adult articles were made "in little" to serve the younger generation. Drop lids on desks fell open to form a writing surface that was usually held in position by a chain support. Many desks had curved legs with a French look. Items from the child's world of yesteryear are fun and a decorative plus to own. Actually, today's younger generation can still use and enjoy them, if their elders permit them to do so.

Child's combination bookcase-desk with desk on left-hand side to accommodate left-handed writer; 32" wide, 13" deep, 56" high. In Illinois, **$695.**

Child's fall-front desk with French-style legs and ribbon decoration on drop lid; 19" wide, 13½" deep, 39" high. In Wisconsin, **$310.**

9 Bedtime Tales

Even as late as the early years of this century, the bedroom was the scene of the entrance of life into the world and the exit from it. There the baby was cradled by motherly arms for the first time, and the sick were nourished. Because the complete cycle of life revolved in the bedroom, it was an important place. Furnishings for it received heavy emphasis. Customers were urged to buy three-piece matching sets. Usually a bed, dresser, and washstand comprised a suite, but cheval dressers and chests of drawers were sold too.

In addition to providing a place to rest, this chamber had another function. Many rural and small town homes of this period did not have plumbing facilities. A supplement to the Saturday night bath in a tub dragged into the kitchen was the popular sponge bath from a bowl in the bedroom. That's where a washstand came in handy as a housing and holding unit. The toilet or chamber set stored in or placed on the stand could consist of twelve matching pieces, if you counted lids separately as catalogs did. The potty for use in sickness or for nighttime emergency urgencies had to have a lid, as did the slop jar in which wastes were carried out to be dumped. The large bowl for washing and the corresponding pitcher dominated the sets. A cup, toothbrush holder, and small pitcher were included. A lidded soap dish counted as three pieces since it had a removable inner drainer. On a cold winter night, the water in a washbasin could freeze, and it was always icy cold to break through the surface to rinse off the face and hands before breakfast. A guest would probably rather fling back the covers in the unheated bedroom and dash downstairs, clothes in hand, to dress as the children did, in warmth and semiprivacy behind the stove. However, this would not have been acceptable behavior.

Two-piece bedroom set: bed, 57" wide, headboard 72" high; dresser with swing mirror, 41" wide, 18" deep, 78½" high. In Wisconsin, **$975** *for the two-piece set.*

Three-piece bedroom set with spoon carving: bed, 54½" wide, headboard 69½" high; dresser with swing mirror, 40½" wide, 18½" deep, 72" high; washstand, 30" wide, 16¼" deep, 29" high, 7" back rail. In Iowa, $1,750 for the three-piece set.

*Three-piece quarter-sawed bedroom set: bed 56" wide, headboard 48" high; washstand with towel bar top, 32" wide, 19" deep, 49½" high; dresser with swing mirror, 44" wide, 22" deep, 66" high. In Wisconsin, **$1,250** for the three-piece set.*

Three-piece bedroom set; bed, 58" wide, headboard 41" high; cheval dresser with hat cabinet and two small drawers, 45" wide, 20" deep, 72" high; washstand, 32" wide, 18" deep, 49" high. In Iowa, $1,500 for the three-piece set.

*Two-piece bedroom set: bed with applied decorations, 60" wide, headboard 78" high; dresser with serpentine front, applied decorations, and swing mirror, 44" wide, 22" deep, 80" high. In Wisconsin, **$1,150** for the two-piece set.*

*Bed with applied decorations; 56½" wide, headboard 65" high. In Iowa, **$545**.*

Bed with applied decorations and roll on footboard, 56½" wide; headboard 46" high. In Illinois, $550.

Washstand; 21½" wide, 15½" deep, 29½" high, 3¼" splashback. In Iowa, $175.

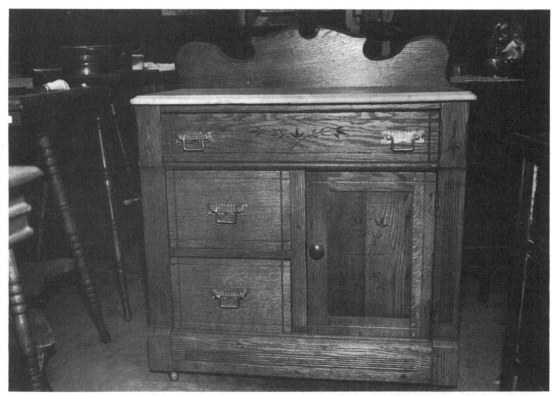

Victorian-style washstand commode with white marble top; 30½" wide, 16¼" deep, 28½" high, 7" splashback. In Wisconsin, $385.

Washstand with roll front drawer and small swing mirror; 38" wide, 19½" deep, 60" high. In Illinois, $425.

Washstand with serpentine projection top drawer; 32" wide, 17" deep, 30" high, 7½" splashback. In Michigan, $310.

Washstand with quarter-sawed serpentine drawer and doors that are veneered; 33" wide, 20" deep, 29½" high. In Illinois, $325.

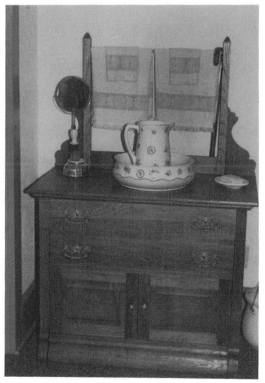

Washstand with towel bar top; 36" wide, 19" deep, 53½" high. In Ohio, $340.

Washstand with towel bar top; 32¹/₂" wide, 16¹/₂" deep, 53¹/₂" high. In Illinois, **$355.**

Washstand with towel bar top; 30¹/₂" wide, 17¹/₂" deep, 54" high. In Iowa, **$355.**

Washstand with applied decorations and serpentine projection drawer; 38" wide, 20" deep, 28¹/₂" high, 4¹/₂" splash-back. In Illinois, **$355.**

Washstand commode with replaced towel bar and ser-pentine drawer front; 32" wide, 19" deep, 51" high. In Iowa, $245.

Princess dresser with swell front; 44" wide, 23" deep, 73" high. In Illinois, $390.

Washstand with combination towel bar-mirror top and intricate paw feet; 30" wide, 21" deep, 68" high. In Indiana, $475.

Washstand with side-by-side towel bar and mirror top; 32" wide, 19" deep, 64" high. In Pennsylvania, $365.

Washstand with side-by-side towel bar and mirror top; 40" wide, 18" deep, 65" high. In Illinois, $410.

Washstand with side-by-side towel bar and mirror top; 34" wide, 19" deep, 68" high. In Pennsylvania, $385.

Lift-top "sick room" commode; 16" square, 16" high. In Ohio, $125.

Dresser with swing mirror; 42" wide, 18½" deep, 73" high. In Illinois, **$395.**

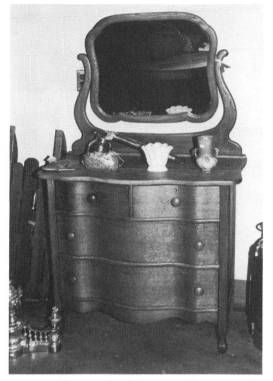

Dresser with serpentine front and swing mirror; 38" wide, 19½" deep, 63" high. In Illinois, **$425.**

Storage space for clothes and personal belongings was necessary. Dressers (bureaus) frequently included a swing mirror that could be tilted for better viewing if one wanted to inspect the face more clearly or see the hem of a dress or the fit of a pair of trousers. In the French language, bureau refers to a study table or desk with drawers for writing supplies. Americans adopted this word to describe a chest of drawers that may or may not have a mirror. Both the words dresser and bureau are used interchangeably by Americans, but dresser has been selected here.

Hotel dresser with applied decorations, swing mirror, and serpentine side drawers; 46½" wide, 23" deep, 71½" high. In Colorado, **$495.**

*Dresser with swing mirror, three roll-front top drawers, three serpentine lower drawers, and paw feet; 44½" wide, 22" deep, 74¼" high. In Iowa, **$495**.*

*Dresser with swing mirror; 38" wide, 18" deep, 69" high. In Iowa, **$395**.*

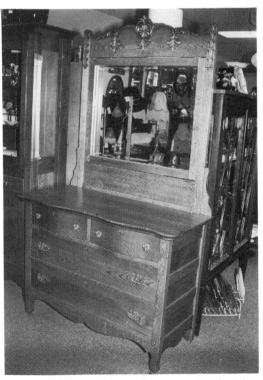

*Dresser with oval swing mirror and applied decorations; 34" wide, 21" deep, 75½" high. In Iowa, **$395**.*

*Dresser with serpentine top drawers and applied decorations on mirror frame; 45" wide, 22" deep, 78" high. In Michigan, **$675**.*

Dresser with serpentine front, swing mirror and applied decorations; 40" wide, 21" deep, 76" high. In Illinois, $565.

Dresser with swing mirror, swell front, and applied leaf garlands on mirror frame; 45" wide, 21" deep, 76¼" high. In Illinois, $495.

Dresser with swing mirror and pressed design at crest; 41½" wide, 19" deep, 69" high. In Michigan, $425.

Dresser with swing mirror and applied decorations on mirror frame; 42" wide, 20" deep, 68½" high. In Iowa, $450.

Cheval (chevalle) dresser with hat cabinet and two small drawers; 42" wide, 18" deep, 81½" high. In Illinois, $545.

Cheval (chevalle) dresser with hat cabinet and two small drawers; 42" wide, 20" deep, 78½" high. In Iowa, $495.

Chiffonier with swell sides, six lower serpentine drawers, and applied decorations; 34" wide, 20" deep, 50" high. In Michigan, $525.

Chiffonier with quarter-sawed oak serpentine front; 33" wide, 19" deep, 48½" high. In Illinois, $525.

In France, a horse is a cheval; thus, a full-length mirror mounted on swivels in a frame becomes a cheval mirror. A tall looking glass above two long, low drawers form a cheval dresser. Often a cupboard was adjacent to the mirror and might serve as a hat cabinet. Drawers could be included.

We dare you to find the word "Jerome" in other oak books. Here's how it came to be. A mother read a story to her little boy about a small lad named Jerome who was an orphan. The fact that the boy in the book was separated from his parents made a deep impression on the youngster. Later he saw the hat cabinet portion of a cheval dresser that had been removed from its normal position to serve as a little stand beside a bed. This isolated, small cabinet without its parent dresser reminded the boy of the lonely lad in the tale. He told his mother, "That's a Jerome." The name stuck, and in her antiques shop, the woman has a Jerome for sale.

A tall, narrow chest of drawers is a chiffonier. A serpentine front is one that ripples in and out much like a snake in motion. A drawer with a roll or a side with a rounding protrusion is spoken of as having a swell front. "Projection top" refers to a case piece that has a drawer that hangs out over its lower section. These styling characteristics show up well on chiffoniers. An expensive version might include a side lock. A key would be needed to unlock the hinged strip of wood that covered one stile (upright framing). When the key was turned, this swung open, unlocking all the doors. When it was closed, none of the drawers could be opened.

Chifforobes are units consisting of a chest of drawers on one side and a narrow wardrobe (space to hang clothes) on the other. They could be made entirely of wood or have a mirror above the drawers. For an additional sum, the door could be covered by a full-length mirror. These were handy in small homes that did not have built-in closets and were adequate when the owner did not possess many garments. Excess clothes could be hung on pegs that lined the walls.

Chiffonier with attached swing mirror and applied decorations; 34" wide, 18½" deep, 63" high. In Illinois, $450.

Chiffonier with attached swing mirror and swell front; 30" wide, 19" deep, 70" high. In Illinois, $495.

133

Chiffonier with serpentine front; 30" wide, 18" deep, 45" high. In Illinois, $310.

Quarter-sawed oak chiffonier with attached swing mirror and scroll feet; 34" wide, 20" deep, 69" high. In Virginia, $325.

Ash hotel chiffonier with attached swing mirror, 30" wide, 17" deep, 63½" high. In Colorado, $495.

Quarter-sawed oak chiffonier with attached swing mirror; 32" wide, 18" deep, 73½" high. In Iowa, $425.

Chiffonier with serpentine front and applied decorations on mirror frame and support; 34" wide, 19" deep, 70" high. In Iowa, **$595.**

Chifforobe with artificial grain to resemble quarter-sawed oak; 44½" wide, 21½" deep, 70½" high. In Virginia, **$245.**

Chifforobe; 43½" wide, 19¼" deep, 67½" high. In Illinois, **$325.**

If a person had many changes of attire, he might own a spacious wardrobe in which to put this generous assortment. Naturally, wardrobes of such proportions would not bend to go through doors or up winding staircases. An ingenious way to overcome this handicap and their heftiness was to make them collapsible. The sides, front, and back could be removed from the base and top and could be reassembled at the site desired. One word of warning. Think! If you move such a piece, mark the individual parts with arrows to indicate which ends goes up, where joining occurs, and the left and right sides. Pertinent information eases and hastens the assembly procedure. Since not all wardrobes can be dismantled, they can be difficult to transport. In addition, a modern home may not accommodate one. For example, a cornice (top decorative molding) may not fit because ceilings have shrunk in height over the years. That's one reason why a measuring tape is a handy companion when one is on the prowl for antiques. Space perception can be deceptive.

During this time period, milady sometimes had a dressing table at which she could sit to brush, comb, and crimp her hair. A curling iron could be

Collapsible or breakdown wardrobe; 51" wide, 17¹/₂" deep, 85" high. In Iowa, **$1,195.**

placed in a kerosene lamp chimney or over a stove burner to heat. If, when it was tested on paper, it left brown char marks, it would singe the hair. Like Papa Bear's porridge in the tale of *Goldilocks and the Three Bears,* it would be too hot to be good. If it was just right like Baby Bear's full bowl, it would be the correct temperature to create a soft wave. Curling irons have been revived, but now they operate with electricity and have buttons that flash red when they are heating.

Wardrobe manufactured by the Marshall Furniture Co. of Henderson, Kentucky, makers of oak wardrobes and cabinets. Two bevel-glass mirrors, pilasters at sides and center, and intricately carved applied decorations, including grotesques (fish-like) flanking crest; 54¹/₂" wide, 20" deep, 102" high. In Wisconsin, **$2,500.**

Wardrobe; 36" wide, 14" deep, 73" high. In Illinois, **$795.**

Wardrobe; 39½" wide, 16" deep, 83" high. In Iowa, $895.

Dressing table with attached swing mirror and swell drawer front; 34½" wide, 19" deep, 60" high. Chair 27" high. In Illinois, $445 for the two-piece set.

Dressing table; 36" wide, 17½" deep, 57" high. In Illinois, $465.

Men had mirrored stands in the bedrooms that assisted them as they drew their sharp, long-stemmed razors across their faces. A place for storing toiletries was included.

Men wore detachable, stand-up collars and cuffs, which were kept stiffly starched. It was an adventure to accompany Dad to the laundry. Nevertheless, it was frightening to walk over the Ashtabula bridge with its deep chasm after hearing stories repeated about the great train wreck when cars plunged into the water far below. To a child, it was such a long span, but with Dad there and by looking across the road, not directly down, it was possible to make it across.

On the downtown side toward the river, tucked way back, was a small shop which housed a Chinese laundry. The owners wore their queues with pride, shuffled in slippers, and had long robes. Their greeting of favored customers was joyous and lilting, but r's were difficult for these newcomers to enunciate. "Hello, Leveland Thulson," was enthusiastic if not accurate as Rev. Thurston exchanged a package of dirty, wilted collars for clean, stiff ones.

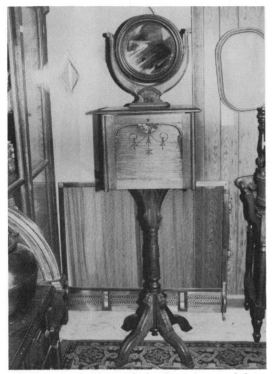

A man needed a special space to place his collar box and a certain site for the collar and cuff buttons that held them in place. Some dressers had drawers designed for these masculine accessories. Each piece of bedroom furniture had a need to meet and a purpose for being.

It is interesting to know that, as the nineteenth century came to a close, white painted, airy iron beds were advertised as being elegant and stylish. Dressers and washstands could be painted with white enamel to match these neat, clean, sanitary beds. Some had brass trim. Solid brass versions were available too. Claims were made that metal beds were outselling wooden types. Times were changing.

Shaving stand with attached swing mirror and drop-front cabinet; 18" wide, 16" deep, 66" high. In Iowa, **$675.**

Mirror that was once a part of a cheval dresser; 22" wide, 52" high. In Wisconsin, **$85.**

Dresser stand; 9" wide, 7" deep, 18½" high. In Iowa, **$135.**

138

10 Accent on Accessories

Antique or collectible accessories — where do you put them? The answer is easy. Anywhere. Display them to your liking.

When inside plumbing was not available in the home (or, for that matter, in stores and office buildings), it was necessary to include grooming articles where they were easily accessible. A hanging comb case frequently included a mirror and was kept near the washbasin, either in the kitchen or the bedroom.

Small hanging cabinets could have towel bars and, in addition to holding soaps, shaving razors, cups, and brushes, might be the storage site for medicinal preparations. A business establishment without plumbing would need a washbowl and pitcher with perhaps a hanging towel and a small supply cabinet. With a bit of imagination, a modern family created an attractive but practical display by combining an oldtime medicine cabinet with a hat rack that now holds guest towels in a bathroom.

Medicine cabinet; 19" wide, 6" deep, 23¼" high. In Illinois, **$195.**

Comb case; 11" wide, 3" deep, 15" high. In Iowa, **$155.**

Comb case with mirror and incised decorations; 14" wide, 4" deep, 24" high. In Colorado, **$125.**

Spice cabinets (or boxes) were used in the kitchen when special seasonings were still bought in hunk or seed form and had to be grated or pulverized at home. A mortar (hard bowl) and pestle (pounder) was kept to grind or mash them. Each drawer was labeled to indicate its contents. Constant touching to remove the desired spices and wiping to clean the surface faded the letters throughout the years. When a box is refinished, the words disappear. It is possible to purchase a decal-type replacement, but some collectors treasure the original more than they do a rejuvenated appearance. Today these spice cabinets turn up almost anywhere. One woman uses hers to hold sewing needs. Another places small waterproof containers in the open drawers to display a couple of tiny growing plants. There isn't a room in the house spiceboxes haven't invaded. Tuck in some velvet and use them for jewelry or guest soaps and make-up. They integrate well with country decors. A spicy odor sometimes clings, and wear is an expected part of vintage ones. Check the signs of age, because examples are being made currently. If you want a box for a special purpose, be sure to notice whether it can rest flat as well as hang, since some have an extension at the base that does not permit them to be set down.

Spice cabinet; 10" wide, 5" deep, 17" high. In Iowa, **$210.**

Plate rail; 22" wide, 2" deep, 10" high. In Iowa, **$145.**

Plate rails are shelves with ridges and perhaps a protective bar that show off attractive china properly in kitchen or dining areas. What better place to expose Grandma's treasured Deldare ware, tea leaf, or Lenox to public view than a plate rail?

The home sewing machine helped many a family dress well. While the earliest patent was issued to an Englishman in 1790, it was not practical. Other versions were developed, but the man who receives the credit for inventing the ancestor of today's machine is Elias Howe. His machine, patented in 1846, was the first practical one sold to customers. Howe's machine was vigorously opposed by hand tailors and seamstresses who resented an invention that reduced their opportunities to find work. In 1854, Isaac Merrit Singer added improvements that included the foot-operated treadle. Singer, the innovator, was also the first to install an electric motor on a sewing machine in 1889.

Clocks are versatile. They are comfortable almost anywhere. Tall cases stand on the floor, while others are designed to hang on walls or sit on shelves or do either. The term mantle clock refers to any type that fills a space on a shelf.

It is said that a clock must be perfectly level or it won't run. Because of this, some intelligent person decided to put a level in a shelf. It seems sometimes that a minor tilt is required. If you have a wall clock, it is a good idea to pencil mark its best operating position so that if it is jarred in dusting it can be correctly returned to its place.

Those marked "regulator" supposedly indicate accuracy in their ability to keep time. Many so labeled were made in Connecticut, a state greatly concerned with creating timepieces. Although there were several thousand makers throughout the nation, Connecticut was a leader. The following are facts about some of the factories that operated in that state.

In this country, until about 1812, clocks were mainly featured in public buildings while, in general, homes had sundials to indicate time. Primarily, it was through the work of one man that inexpensive clocks became affordable to the masses. "He's crazy! It can't be done," his

Singer sewing machine; 35" wide, 17" deep, 30½" high. In Illinois, **$110.**

contemporaries must have muttered. They knew Eli Terry had accepted a contract to produce four thousand clocks in three years at four dollars each. This was outlandish in a day when every clock was individually made to order by hand. For Terry's purposes, crafted brass parts were too expensive, so, in 1807, he created machines and tools to produce identical wooden parts. He established an assembly line so each worker put in one of these interchangeable pieces. By introducing mass production to the industry, Terry completed four thousand clocks that the public could afford to buy. He made a shelf type that peddlers on horse or mule back could transport with ease. Before that they saved weight and space by selling the works only, and the purchaser was responsible for creating a case. If none was made and the buyer hung up the face and pendulum, it formed a version that was dubbed a "wag-on-the-wall" clock. Other members of Terry's family joined the firm and operated it throughout the 1800s.

Waterbury regulator clock; 16" wide, 4½" deep, 37" high. In Iowa, **$425.**

Clock shelf with built-in level; 14½" wide, 4¼" deep, 6¼" high. In Illinois, **$165.**

Dating of Terry clocks is possible by looking up the various company names that changed as the partnerships switched. For a quick method, in 1831 the post office address was Terrysville in honor of Eli Junior. In 1872, the "s" was deleted to make Terryville. An Eli Terry clock would be pre-1872 if it said Terrysville and after that date if the "s" is missing.

Seth Thomas was a carpenter who began working for Eli Terry in 1808, and who later became a partner. In 1818, he bought a Terry patent and set up a shop of his own at Plymouth Hollow. His name became as tightly affixed to clocks of the era as the paper labels glued inside their backs. These papers listed the manufacturer, offered care and operating instructions, and presumably helped keep dust out. The town was renamed Thomaston in 1866 in his honor, so Plymouth Hollow labels precede that date.

From the inception of its clock factory in about 1802, Waterbury, Connecticut, grew to become the brass and copper works center of the world. Around 1839, brass parts could be stamped out, so inexpensive metal parts became a reality, and the wooden ones that had replaced costly handcrafted brass types became passé.

Ansonia shelf clock with pressed designs on case; 15" wide, 23" high. In Alaska, **$325.**

Tampa calendar clock made by the New Haven Clock Co.; 14" wide, 4½" deep, 22" high. In Iowa, **$395.**

Ansonia wall clock; 13½" wide, 6½" deep, 55" high. In Iowa, $415.

Gilbert calendar wall or shelf clock; 14" wide, 4" deep, 28½" high. In Iowa, $325.

About 1851, at Ansonia, the Ansonia Clock Company was founded as a subsidiary of the brass company there to produce quality products. Late in the 1870s, the shop was moved to New York City where it functioned until Russia bought its machinery in 1930.

Others, all Connecticut based, include the New Haven Clock Company of New Haven and William F. Gilbert's Company of Winsted. The Ingraham Clock Company in Bristol, established by Elias Ingraham (1805-1885) created cases with classical designs, often with pillars.

Rules to observe or care tips for clocks:

- Retain labels.
- Remove the pendulum when moving a clock so parts do not get bent.
- When moving, pack or remove weights so they don't bang and do damage.
- Some clocks wind to the right, some to the left.
- The speed of the clock depends on the length of the pendulum. Lower slower; higher sprier.
- Clock repair dates are often written on the back and are of interest.
- Beware of brads in clock cases. This is a contemporary method of construction. Some signs of wear should also be present.

Another accessory of old adopted today is the wooden telephone. Alexander Graham Bell was a teacher who was concerned with the problems of deaf people, including his wife. He was also an inventor who, on March 10, 1876, developed the telephone. The first words transmitted were said to his assistant in the next room, "Mr. Watson, come here. I want you!"

Three months later, Bell exhibited this discovery at the Centennial Exposition in Philadelphia. The public enjoyed the "toy" without expressing much interest. In 1877, a farsighted banker erected the first commercial telephone line, which extended three miles and connected his home with his bank in Boston. That same year, the Bell Company was founded by a group of men.

When some New York City businesses first installed phones, they advertised the fact to indicate they were progressive. Now such communication is not considered a novelty but a necessity.

In the beginning, boys were hired to operate telephone switchboards, but gradually women took over these tasks. Turning the crank on an old wooden box caused "Central" (the operator) to answer, "Number please." If someone were on your own party line, you could call direct, not by dial but by crank. A long twist of the handle combined with short ones provided a code. A person's ring might be two longs and two shorts, for example. Others on the line could quietly lift the receiver to eavesdrop, so neighbors were quick to know about the activities of others. Sometimes the third listener might butt in and take over the conversation. It was never wise to prattle loosely on a party line.

People occasionally update these phones so they can function once again. When the insides are gutted (alas, there goes value, purists protest), they can house radios or provide a slight bit of cabinet space. Communication through two longs and two shorts has rung its way into the past, taking "Central" and her "Number please" along, but the old phones linger on. Functional items of yesteryear are treasures today.

Ingraham wall or shelf clock; 15" wide, 4¼" deep, 29" high. In Ohio, **$425.**

Wall telephone; 8½" wide, 18" high. In Illinois, **$310.**

Wall telephone. In Ohio, **$395.**

Wall telephone. In Wisconsin, $325.

Wall telephone. In Wisconsin, $295.

Wall telephone. In Iowa, $325.

Medicine cabinet; 17" wide, 7" deep, 18" high, 4½" back rail. In Wisconsin, $175.

Medicine cabinet; 16" wide, 6" deep, 27" high. In Michigan, $195.

Hanging corner cabinet; 18½" wide, 8½" deep, 26" high. In Colorado, $225.

Spice cabinet; 11" wide, 5½" deep, 17½" high. In Wisconsin, $195.

147

Spice cabinet; 11" wide, 5" deep, 13½" high. In Illinois,
$195.

Fire screen with needlepoint picture; 23" wide, 26" high.
In Iowa, **$125.**

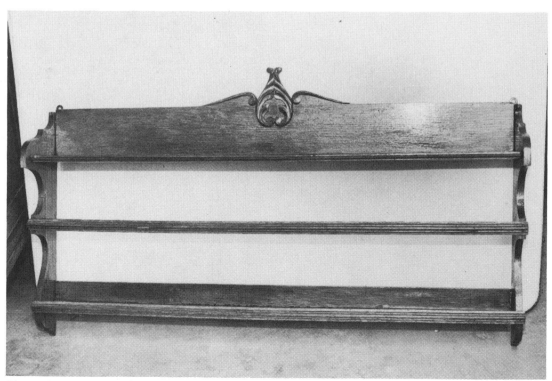

Plate rail; 36" wide, 5½" deep, 20" high. In Iowa, **$155.**

Plate rail; 38¹/₂" wide, 4¹/₂" deep, 14¹/₂" high. In Illinois, **$165.**

Sewing machine cabinet; 24" wide, 18" deep, 31" high. In Illinois, **$155.**

Sewing machine cabinet; 24" wide, 16¹/₂" deep, 30¹/₄" high. In Iowa, **$165.**

Sewing machine cabinet; 32" wide, 18" deep, 31" high. In Illinois, $255.

Waterbury wall clock with brass weights; 14" wide, 5" deep, 36" high. In Iowa, $1,650.

Gilbert shelf clock; 17" wide, 4" deep, 24¼" high. In Iowa, $350.

Wall clock; 14½" wide, 4" deep, 36" high. In Iowa, $495.

Wall clock with weights; 10″ wide, 5″ deep, 33″ high. In Ohio, **$450.**

Octagonal school-type wall clock; 17″ wide at face, 3½″ deep, 30″ high. In Pennsylvania, **$450.**

Octagonal school-type wall clock; 18″ wide at face, 3½″ deep, 32″ high. In Ohio, **$450.**

Wall mirror; 22″ wide, 45½″ high. In Ohio, **$156.**

Multilinear framed mirror; 27" wide, 29" high. In Illinois, $135.

Frame with gold inner and outer outline; 22" diameter. In Illinois, $45.

Mission-style tea cart with black stamp on bottom reading, "Stickley Bros., Co., Grand Rapids"; 17" wide, 28" long, 29" high. In Alaska, $450.

*Multilinear frame alternating with gilt on oak easel; 29½" × 33½". In Illinois, **$145** for easel, **$180** for framed picture.*

*Multilinear oak-gilt frame; 24" × 27". In Illinois, **$145**.*

*Frame with gilt inner lining holding Paul Norton print of Prospect Park, Moline, Illinois; 25" × 21". In Illinois, **$155**.*

11   They're Adopted

What's a drugstore? That's a place where prescriptions are filled. Visitors from other lands are amazed at times because most American stores of this type are multifaceted. They may sell souvenirs, toys, cosmetics, sunglasses, socks, shoes, films, cameras, cards, candy, foods, and the list continues. The old term apothecary means pharmacist or druggist, and his shop dispensed medicines exclusively.

In the first half of the 1900s many American drugstores had lunch counters and/or soda fountains. Ice cream tables and chairs might also be found in drugstores if space permitted. Of course, there were confectioners who used these furnishings also.

Red and white, candy-cane-like striped poles used to proclaim, "Hey! I'm a barber shop. Come on in!" The name was derived from the Latin *barba* meaning beard, and early barbers were surgeons too. A law passed while Henry VIII was King of England (1509-1547) terminated this dual role. Barbers were banned from practicing surgery. The symbol on the sign persisted, however. The white spiral stripes represent the bandage the barber wrapped around the patient after bleeding the patient. It was a standard medical practice for many years to open a vein and remove blood to cure illness. In 1799 George Washington's physician bled the dying president in an effort to assist him. Perhaps barbers discarded this sign because they did not like to be reminded of their profession's gory past.

Turn-of-the-century men found companionship in these tonsorial parlors. Special cabinets held shaving supplies and towels. Steady customers each owned a personal shaving mug with fancy designs. There were occupational versions depicting a butcher, doctor, or minister's tasks; and the patron's name or "Father" might be inscribed. Such shaving mugs are highly collectible as decorative accessories for today's home.

Apothecary case; 24" wide, 4" deep, 24" high. In Wisconsin, **$240.**

There was a time when barbers also pulled teeth. The advancement in dental techniques caused the two vocations to separate, even though their chairs remained similar in structure for many years. Both barber chairs and those from old dental offices now rate as household objects.

*Ice cream table with metal frame and claw and ball feet; 25" square, 29" high. In Iowa, **$285.***

*Barbershop case in two pieces; 29½" wide, 23½" deep at base, 74" high. In Colorado, **$515.***

Close-up of metal head on the corner of the apron on the ice cream table.

*Portable dental cabinet in case; 14½" wide, 9½" deep, 14" high. In Iowa, **$250.***

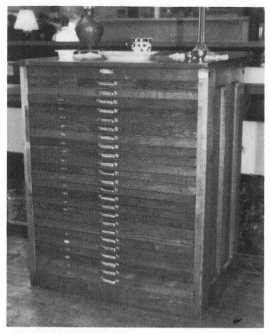

Hamilton printer's cabinet made in Two Rivers, Wisconsin; 65" wide, 24½" deep, 44" high. In Georgia, **$795.**

Drawers from printers' cabinets are being converted into display units for tiny treasures. Some of the slats can be removed to form a slightly larger section. They make fine memory boxes for newlyweds or splendid gifts for anniversary celebrants when filled with meaningful mementos. Items such as a tiny doll, watch, jackknife, miniature pictures of the happy twosome, a model of their black puppy, "their car," a figurine of a teacher or carpenter to represent a profession, or a wee Bible might be chosen. A few spaces may be left for the recipients to add their own special or secret, shared mementos. It's a thoughtful gift given in love, which is special when hung in a wall grouping.

A few generations ago, small-town stores used display cases. They are being rescued by new owners to create an atmosphere with vintage flavor in restaurants or homes. Some homeowners seek to revive the country store in their recreational areas. They frequently include string and brown wrapping paper holders that predate the manufactured paper (or later, plastic) bags. Merchants wrapped packages for people. The stoves the men checker players loafed around in the winter, the cracker barrels, and coffee bins are becoming parts of home decors. The stoves may be functioning again as energysavers, while the barrels and bins become hampers.

Store display case; 72½" wide, 18¼" deep, 35½" high. In Illinois, **$1,150.**

One much enjoyed relic from the past is the spool cabinet. Examples serve as coffee tables or at the ends of sofas. They hold jewelry and scarves on dressers. Did you ever wonder what the initials O.N.T. stand for on Clark cabinets? Actually, their prosaic meaning is "Our New Thread." Wonder what held their "old" thread? Many versions of spool cabinets are available, ranging from those with desk tops to models with a series of drawers with dividers inside. They were supplied by manufacturers as display cases for their products. One type permitted spools to be inserted in slots in rows according to size and color by pushing open a swinging lid on the top. Knobs pivoted a revolving mechanism so all the types could be seen, and the selected spool could be extracted through a door at the base. Since spool cabinets usually were placed on counters, a woman could gaze into the mirror as she held a bit of fabric to her face to decide whether the color or pattern was flattering. If one should be on the floor and had a looking glass, a shoe buyer could inspect his feet. Because general stores in farm communities were diversified, they carried everything from soap to suits. The ghost of the country store is emerging again in both homes and businesses.

Blauls Better Brand Beans (B.B.B.B.) Coffee box with hinged dropdown lid; 24" wide, 22½" deep, 32" high. In Colorado, **$250.**

Merrick's Six Cord Cotton spool cabinet dated July 20, 1897, with two revolving spool dispensors flanking the mirror (the thread weights range from 8 to 100); 31½" wide, 17¼" deep, 23½" high. In Illinois, **$975.**

Shoe store footstool with twisted metal legs; 10" wide, 25" long, 14" high. In Illinois, $65.

Hanging water fountain from a Mississippi riverboat with a towel-bar side. Behind the framed glass on the face was placed the scheduled stops along the Mississippi; 11" wide, 9" deep, 28" high. In Colorado, $395.

Occasionally a newspaper will feature a story about the last railroad train that will chug along a certain track into a specified town. Airplanes now flash across the continent carrying mail that used to be sorted by postal employees as they sped along in railroad cars. Stations are boarded up or have been converted to eating establishments. No longer is the Iron Horse the force it once was. In 1830, the first regular train service in the United States was inaugurated in South Carolina. On May 10, 1869, the race to complete the first transcontinental railroad ended when a golden spike was driven through the last linking rail when the eastern and western sections met. Wires informed the entire nation. People shouted and celebrated. East and West were no longer twain.

Transportation is different now. The riverboat and ocean liner are akin to the old gray mare. The song says, "She ain't what she used to be." Boats and ships no longer attract the passengers or freight they once did, but their furnishings and fixtures are avidly sought by collectors.

The three-hundred-and-fifty-mile Erie Canal connected Buffalo on Lake Erie to Albany on the Hudson River. Its success caused canal fever to spread to other states, and Illinois almost went bankrupt in its efforts to finance the "big ditches."

Mark Twain's Mississippi River held allure. People ran to the shore to watch the steamboats approach. Boys idolized that special being, the riverboat pilot, and dreamed of becoming one when they grew up. He was better than the captain of the crew, and his uniform was splendid. But that glamorous era faded into history too. Only the tales and the tokens linger.

On Sunday in bygone years, bells rang out joyfully to beckon parishioners and remind them it was time to come and worship. "The Little Brown Church" near Nashua, Iowa, was immortalized in a hymn when William S. Pitts viewed and wrote about the site. Now it attracts thousands of visitors. As the verse says, "No spot is so dear to my childhood." Ecclesiastical mementos, especially those from one's own dear church, attract many. Old stained glass windows are incorporated into homes, but perhaps the easiest item to adopt is a pew to serve as a seat in a casual area. Occupational and store articles can become decorative assets. Why not adopt one?

Two church pews with applied decorations and impressed design on ends; 48" wide, 20" deep, 40" high. In Iowa, $375 each.

Hanging wall cabinet with drawer was a free gift from Koch if you purchased the complete barbershop fixtures from them; 14½" wide, 7" deep, 21" high. In Colorado, $325.

Bentwood ice cream chair; 33" high. In Illinois, $85.

Bentwood barbershop chair; 38" high. In Illinois, **$125.**

Bentwood barbershop armchair; 23½" arm to arm, 41" high. In Illinois, **$145.**

Dental cabinet; 29½" wide, 14½" deep, 60½" high. In Colorado, **$1,250.**

Dental cabinet with brass pulls; 39" wide, 15½" deep, 33½" high. In Ohio, **$1,200.**

Dental cabinet with two rolltops, applied decorations, and brass hardware; 33½" wide, 18½" deep, 30" high. In Iowa, **$1,750.**

Showcase from early 1900s Alaskan jewelry store with ten drawers accessible in back; 72" wide, 24" deep, 41" high. In Alaska, **$1,295.**

161

Jeweler's desk with glass pulls; 36" wide, 20" deep, 39" high. In Illinois, $675.

Store display case with two sliding doors; 34" wide, 10" deep, 34¹/₂" high. In Wisconsin, $285.

Hardware store display case; 32" wide, 14" deep at bottom, 6" deep at top, 50¹/₂" high. In Iowa, $320.

Revolving spice dispenser made by the G.E. Stewart Co., Mfgrs., Norwalk, Ohio, patented June 20, 1901, and supplied by them to McFadden Coffee & Spice Co., Dubuque, Iowa (the other side holds ginger, mustard, and pepper); 14¹/₂" wide, 8" deep, 29" high. In Wisconsin, $245.

Spool cabinet; 24" wide, 16½" deep, 17½" high. In Iowa, **$595.**

Crowley's Needle cabinet; 19" wide, 9½" deep, 9½" high. In Iowa, **$350.**

163

Time clock manufactured in Endicott, New York, by International Time Recording, which today is I.B.M.; 13½″ wide, 10″ deep, 40″ high. In Iowa, $525.

Time clock manufactured by The Cincinnati Time Recording Co., Cincinnati, Ohio; 13½″ wide, 7″ deep, 35″ high. In Illinois, $465.

Watchmaker's cabinet; 20½″ wide, 6½″ deep, 12½″ high. In Illinois, $475.

Dental cabinet; 26" wide, 11" deep at top and 17" at base, 60" high. In Illinois, **$975.**

Hanging wall cabinet from a church; 29½" wide, 7½" deep, 28" high. In Iowa, **$325.**

Mission-style shoe shine bench; 65" wide, 21" deep, 48" high. In Iowa, **$325.**

Church pew; 52" wide, 19" deep, 35" high. In Iowa, **$325.**

Nine-drawer stack file cabinet manufactured by Yawman & Erbe Mfg. Co., Rochester, New York; 33" wide, 18" deep, 17½" high. In Wisconsin, **$265.**

Six-drawer file cabinet manufactured by Yawman & Erbe Mfg. Co., Rochester, New York; 11¼" wide, 15" deep, 14½" high. In Iowa, $225.

Six-stack file cabinet; 13¼" wide, 15" deep, 29½" high. In Iowa, $425.

Four-drawer file cabinet; 14½" wide, 24½" deep, 52" high. In Iowa, $495.

Combination bookcase-file cabinet dated 1903, used either in a library or office; 41" wide, 17" deep, 60" high. In Wisconsin, $1,295.

*Sixteen-drawer library card catalog file; 14¹/₂" wide, 20" deep, 52" high. In Colorado, **$525.***

Close-up showing how each section of the card catalog file can be removed from its case.

*Pool ball rack; 23¹/₂" wide, 4¹/₄" deep, 19¹/₂" high. In Wisconsin, **$150.***

*Baker's cabinet from Elmyra, New York; 50¹/₂" wide, 26¹/₂" deep, 28¹/₂" high. In Georgia, **$850.***

12   Men of Vision

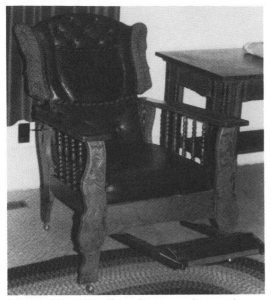

Morris chair with pull-out footrest and pressed carving; 30½" arm to arm, 39" high. Not oak. In Iowa, **$250.**

Cane seat chair with an incised bird and flower design in the back rail—an example of Eastlake's rectangular, plain lines; 34" high. In Colorado, **$125.**

They were crusaders, just as surely as King Richard the Lion-Hearted and his knights who marched against the infidels in Jerusalem. They fought shoddy, overly ornate machine workmanship. Who were these men? They were promoters of, or were influenced by, the Arts and Crafts Movement that originated in England. A revival of interest in the decorative arts began about 1875, but the actual reaction to over embellishment occurred about ten years later. Artistic leaders in other countries expressed a similar dislike for the tasteless eclecticism (the copying, adapting, and combining of motifs and forms from previous periods) that existed in furniture manufactured in the late 1800s. They rebelled. They wanted to stress handcrafted articles. "Back to basics." "Back to simplicity," they demanded.

The Industrial Revolution created new jobs and a new class of workers — the middle class. Mass production reduced the cost of many articles, ownership of which had been restricted to the wealthy in the past. The vast majority of the public had purchasing power as inexpensive wares became available. The Arts and Crafts Movement was not widely embraced, but it did cause various people to modify their thinking. Decorators, for example, began to discard cluttered interiors in favor of the clean, orderly look for homes that the Arts and Crafts Movement advocates endorsed.

A few of the leaders of the movement were John Ruskin, William Morris, and Charles Lock (Locke) Eastlake of England who influenced Elbert Hubbard and Gustav Stickley of the United States. These men were not clones. They dared to differ. Was it the wealthy, religiously inclined John Ruskin (1819-1900) who instigated the Arts and Crafts Movement? If this altruistic man was not the founder, at least he was an active proponent. It was his tenet that all work must meet three requirements. It should be useful, cheerful, and honest. London-born Ruskin grew up in an affluent home and became a professor at prestigious Oxford University. Teaching was his profession, but his concerns were distributed generously about. He was a dedicated social reformer, art critic, and writer. Because of his belief in biblical doctrines of caring and sharing, he used much of his inherited money to improve the conditions of the poor. In addition, Ruskin opined that quality architecture was next of kin to morality and therefore was related to religion. Because he sought quality, many authorites believe his writings and discussions did help promote change.

John Ruskin and William Morris (1834-1896) were in accord in various matters. They believed that an article's artistic worth could not be judged by its cost or because it was considered fashionable. They felt that only utilitarian or beautiful objects should be in a home. Morris was an artist, architect, and poet who researched church history as a college student and later established a firm that specialized in ecclesiastical furnishings. The company produced stained glass windows, murals, tapestries, and wood carvings. When the business expanded, carpets, furniture, metalwork, and book binding were added to the services and products offered. Morris proclaimed, "Real art is the expression by man of his pleasure in labor." He committed himself to hard work and developing the arts. He is commonly remembered for another contribution — the invention of a recliner called a

Morris chair. These chairs featured rods in back which could be moved and placed in various grooves to determine the degree of incline sought. A simple wooden frame held loose cushions that formed the padded seat and backrest. English furniture tended toward a conservative line as a result of William Morris's emphasis on honest workmanship and direct designs. He said simple lines were best.

Charles Lock (or Locke) Eastlake (1836-1906), an architect, felt that the majority of the machined furniture available in the 1860s was deficient in both style and strength. Since Eastlake believed that furnishings should be compatible with the physical structure of the house itself, he began to design the furniture for the homes he built. He decreed that curves wasted wood, were not strong structurally, and were lacking in comfort. His book, *Hints on Household Taste, Furnishings, Upholstery, and Other Details,* stated his beliefs. This volume was published around 1868, but its influence did not sail across the Atlantic until the 1870s.

Close-up of the incised design in the back rail of the Eastlake chair.

Parlor table with the incised lines characteristic of Eastlake; 30" wide, 21½" deep, 30" high. In Iowa, $265.

Larkin china cabinet; 34" wide, 15" deep, 56" high. In Colorado, $450.

Eastlake liked plain, simple squares, rectangles, and other geometric shapes, and he realized that machines could be used to produce quality furniture that was also well designed. He chose oak (or occasionally ash, its lookalike) from which to construct his boxy styles. Many factories in the United States seized his straight lines and gleefully piled them with the excessive decoration Eastlake sought to avoid. While the styles, supposedly similar to his, that America's homemakers bought were not precisely the plain packages Eastlake advocated, a change in tastes did gradually evolve. Seven-foot-high bed headboards shrank, partly from necessity, since America's virgin forests were becoming depleted, and partly from the desire of consumers for something new. Curves, scrolls, flowers, and carvings with exaggerated frills became passé. Lighter furniture in both color and form gradually became fashionable.

While Eastlake was active in England, John D. Larkin established a company in 1875 that bore his name. By 1892, it became the Larkin Soap Manufacturing Company. For a time Larkin's brother-in-law, Elbert Hubbard (1856-1915) was a member of his creative staff. In addition to being an author, Hubbard was an advertising agent whose skill rivaled that of ballyhoo artist P. T. Barnum. Hubbard was equally successful as a promoter. He developed a premium plan based on purchases and created organizations for housewives. They were urged to get their friends together to form Larkin Clubs. The more relatives and acquaintances they could convince to try Larkin products, the more points they could earn. The soap products promoted cleanliness, but the furniture, rugs, silverware, curtains, lamps, and linens were bonus features that kept club members buying. Some furniture was made by Larkin at Buffalo, New York. Most, however, was purchased from other furniture manufacturers.

Today many people erroneously believe that all Larkin desks were meticulously straight of line. They call any plain little fall-front parlor style "Larkin." Oh, is that a mistake. Some truly graceful furnishings came from the Larkin factory and they were widely distributed. Once a dealer had a genteel golden oak china cabinet that seemed to say, "I'm quality." When he was asked if it was a Larkin, he denied it. "They only made straight lines," he replied. If you wish to prove that this is untrue, consult page one-hundred and twenty-two in our *American Oak Furniture Styles and Prices*, Book I. The quiet simplicity is there to create a tastefully executed furnishing. It's a Larkin. The label says so. The premiums Hubbard used as an enticement included those with class.

In the early 1890s, when Elbert Hubbard visited England, he became a convert to the Arts and Crafts Movement and accepted William Morris's rejection of machines. After he returned to Buffalo, he left his brother-in-law's company to establish a colony for handicraft artisans at East Aurora, New York, in about 1895. They were the Roycrofters, who produced products marked Roycroft. They bound books, fashioned pottery, worked with metal, tooled leather, created jewelry, and wove textiles. Later, the furniture they made took on the straight-lined, stolid look similar to that of Gustav Stickley design.

Europe was at war in 1915, and German submarines patrolled the seas. For strategic reasons, they sank ships indiscriminately in the Atlantic waters. The *S.S. Lusitania* was one of their victims on May 7. An American protest could not bring back lost lives. There were one-hundred twenty-eight or one-hundred twelve American casualties among the one-thousand one-hundred and ninety-eight who perished aboard the ship. Accounts vary. At any rate, Elbert Hubbard was a passenger aboard the *Lusitania*, and the leader of the Roycrofters never returned to East Aurora. Years after his death, his influence on the Larkin organization lingered. In 1925, as a part of the observance of their fiftieth anniversary, the company sent out free catalogs that listed Larkin's enticing array of household products. The premiums offered to club members were itemized. Hubbard's advertising ability served his brother-in-law long and well.

The Roycroft symbol found on the base of a brass jardeniere.

Arts and Crafts Movement cupboard attributed to Roy-croft by its owner; 36" wide, 12" deep, 85½" high. In Ohio, **$1,195.**

Larkin chiffonier that has an "information" label on the back (see text for facsimile of label); 33½" wide, 17½" deep, 47½" high. In Iowa, **$495.**

The Larkin Company provided specific instructions to customers who received their furniture as premiums. The following is an example of a label found on the back of a Larkin-made article of furniture.

Helpful information. Atmospheric conditions and changes encountered by furniture while in transit &, often, in the home cause new wood to swell, so the doors & drawers bind & stick.

In the winter the dry heat in the house will generally prove a sufficient remedy within a few weeks & it is better to avoid dressing down the wood, because it is designed to fit perfectly when dry. In the humidity of the summer, however, if the months when the house shall again be heated seem too distant to wait for a natural shrinkage, anyone with a good plane may with intelligent care dress the parts that bind just enough to make action free. But never put the plane on drawers until first you have withdrawn them from the case, inverted them & examined lower-edge of front, also the tops of stationary rails between drawers, for possible excess of varnish which should be scraped off with knife or glass. Before planing a door-edge apply a screw driver to the hinge screws to make sure that they were driven quite in so the hinges entirely close, examine all four edges of door, particularly the hinged edge for excessive varnish. Often, lubrication of the bearing points with Sweet Home Soap is all that is required.

EVERY new piece of furniture should be given a liberal application of Larkin Furniture Polish to remove any chafing, scratches, & the dust of travel.

Drawer pulls, casters & all trimmings, if any, will be found, packaged, in a drawer if any. Key will be found attached to outside of case.

To open a drawer that sticks. Place against the corner-post of case at end of drawer, a small block of wood over a heavy pad of paper. Strike block a sharp blow with a hammer. Repeat this at each end alternately until drawer will open. Larkin, Buffalo, N.Y. Factory #19

If you have any occasion to write us about it, mention this number without fail. Do not cause useless delay for inquiry, by neglecting this. Preserve all crating material until all possibility of reshippment of this article is past.

This is the label from the back of a Larkin chiffonier.

This certifies that this article leaves our hands in perfect condition throughout. It has been carefully inspected by our own special inspector before packed for shipment at the factory where manufactured. If it arrives damaged in any way, it has become so in transit. In writing us about it do not fail to have R. R. agent to endorse on paid freight bill a statement of the condition of the article when delivered to you, and send it to us. Also inform us Factory's No. which appears on another label. (*Imprinted below this in a circle*): Inspector's Seal Larkin Soap Co., Buffalo, N.Y.

Another man influenced by the English Arts and Crafts Movement was Gustav Stickley (1857-1942). This farm lad, one of five brothers, lived a simple life in rural Minnesota. Traditionally, children were co-workers on operating farms. On winter mornings, they would be awakened before daybreak to help with the chores. Both before and after school, they watered the animals, measured the required amount of grain into the feedbins, pitched straw down from the barn loft, or milked the cows. They hauled firewood for ravenous stoves or worked in other ways in the cooperative effort to earn the family living. Through this training, Gustav Stickley learned to perform duties well, in the best, most natural manner possible.

Later he worked in the furniture industry. When he grew in experience and his brothers were older, they joined together and formed the Stickley Brothers Company listed at the Grand Rapids Public Library as one of the more than eighty-five firms which began businesses in this Michigan city from about 1880 to 1900. They manufactured the typical walnut furniture, with appendages and doodads, that was popular in the closing years of the 1800s. Many of the companies did not last long. After all, it was not the most opportune time because the native forests in that area were dwindling rapidly.

Stickley severed his Grand Rapids' relationships in the mid-1890s. He and a partner established a shop near Syracuse, New York, soon afterward. In 1898 Stickley visited England, where he must have been impressed by the Arts and Crafts Movement. On his return, he began to experiment with straight, strong construction in furniture. It was not his intention to create an entirely new furniture style that would be hailed by some critics as an American first, a truly native American style, but that's what he did. He strove for two years to perfect both the forms and finishes until he felt ready to exhibit his designs at the Grand Rapids Furniture Exposition in 1900 and again at the Pan-American Exposition the following year. How gratified he was that his efforts found favor.

Larkin chiffonier that has a "perfect condition" label on the back (see text); 34" wide, 18" deep, 47½" high. In Illinois, $495.

Mission oak arm rocker made by Limbert Arts Crafts Furniture of Grand Rapids and Holland, Michigan; 27¼" arm to arm, 33½" high. In Wisconsin, $175.

Close-up of mark found on mission rocker.

Bookcase with arched apron, a style used by Harvey Ellis, who worked for Stickley from 1903 to 1904; 48" wide, 12" deep, 51" high. In Virginia, **$400.**

One of his designers from 1903 to 1904 was the gifted architect, Harvey Ellis, who tended to add gentle, light, and graceful touches to Stickley's straight, stocky slats. Ellis liked to break up the strict horizontals by using an arch on the apron of tables or chests. Color was added by inserting inlays. His untimely death occurred one short year after he joined Stickley.

Stickley found white oak to be beautiful yet strong. He liked the pronounced flakes revealed when the lumber was quarter sawed, but he felt the pale wood needed the softened, darkened appearance of age to make it more attractive. He experimented with finishes that would enhance and beautify the wood as well as protect it from dirt and stains. He sought a method to cloak his new furniture in the patina that, hitherto, only age could produce.

Since oak has wide-open pores, its absorbing qualities could be increased further by wetting its surface. Assembled furniture was placed in an airtight area where it was exposed to strong ammonia vapors for a certain period of time (perhaps two days), depending on the depth of darkness desired. (A magazine article of the period suggested burning straw to smoke the wood dark, so techniques differed.) Sandpapering for smoothness followed. Stickley experimented with finishes until he attained several shades of brown and a silver gray. After Stickley looked at his work, he found that it was good. He was pleased. He felt it would endure both physically and in popularity.

Have you ever tried to force the wrong letter into a crossword puzzle? It won't work and distorts the whole section. In a similar way, one discordant note could upset the entire home, apparently. All had to chain link together to fit as a complete whole so everything had to be of Craftsman design. In order to acquire the total look, Stickley urged families to have unpretentious houses with his strict, slatted furniture inside. He had a formula he followed. First he built his sturdy, stocky dressers or sideboards. Glittering, golden oak, pressed brass drawer pulls and fancy escutcheons (ornamental plates to encircle keyholes) were deemed out of place. He designed functional hardware of brass, copper, and iron, darkening it to give an old appearance. Hinges and pulls were large, simple yet showy accents.

Mission oak bookcase with mullions on doors, mortise and tenon construction on bottom and top of stiles, and the arched apron, characteristic of Harvey Ellis; 46½" wide, 13" deep, 50½" high. In Wisconsin, **$695.**

Mission oak hall tree showing the flakes of quarter-sawed oak; 26½" wide, 19" deep, 76" high. In Iowa, **$595.**

Mission oak library desk; 49" wide, 30½" deep, 30" high. In Wisconsin, **$295.**

177

Mission oak server or buffet with a fumed finish; 40″ wide, 20″ deep, 37¼″ high, 8½″ rail. In Iowa, $295.

Mission oak sewing rocker with leather seat and pull-out compartment for sewing supplies; 32″ high. In Illinois, $185.

Next the coverings required attention. His firm tanned rich leather with either a hard or soft feel for seats, cushions, and inserts on table tops. Their sheepskin was of highest quality. For door hangings, upholstery, and pillow covers, a canvas of woven jute and flax was recommended in muted earthen tones in red, green, or brown hues. Embroidery and appliqués added attractive dimensions. Versatile linen could be coarse and rough or more gently woven, depending on its intended purpose. Bedspreads and dresser scarves were a part of the total look. Naturally, all of the fabrics had long-wearing endurance or they would not qualify as Craftsman products.

Metal accessories had to harmonize. What would a fireplace be like without stout Craftsman tools? Planters, trays, and chafing dishes should have a plain look that blended. The fancy lights available through other manufacturers did not measure up. Stickley creations featured glass and metal combinations offered in either gas or electric models.

Also, if you liked wicker to mix with and lighten the heavy aspects of oak, willow furniture — in the Stickley manner — was available. Many types of furnishings bore the Craftsman label.

All of this quality was intended for a simple bungalow, a house which Stickley, the architect, designed. What a joy this house was bound to be. After living in a flat or apartment where facilities were often shared, what could be better than having a small place of one's own? The exterior featured a rectangular or square porch, which frequently had squared pillars made of concrete with rocks sunk into the surface. Here families could congregate in cool comfort on hot nights. It also sheltered people from rain or snow as they fumbled for their key to unlock the entry door. Room size was large enough to accommodate necessities, not accumulations. In a bedroom, it might be necessary to sit on a bed in order to pull open the drawers of a dresser.

Mission oak clock; 12" wide, 5" deep, 25" high. In Iowa,
$150.

*Umbrella stand with mission lines; 9" × 9½", 26½"
high. In Iowa,* **$110.**

Upholstered sofa with tufted back; 44" arm to arm, 21" deep, 32½" high. In Illinois, **$235.**

Built-in bookcase, one of the features of the early bungalows; 35½" wide, 42½" high. In Illinois, **$375.**

Built-in cabinet taken from a home designed in mission style; 32" wide, 15" deep, 57½" high. In Iowa, **$395.** *Gilbert clock,* **$225.**

Built-ins were a must. Bookcases, usually one on each side in perfect balance, flanked the fireplace. A boxy window seat was the just-right spot to kitten-curl with a book. Exposed beams overhead and wainscoting (paneling on the lower part of the walls) offered a warm wood look. Stickley sincerely believed and fervently preached that such homes would influence the moral fiber of its occupants favorably. People would be better citizens because of the clean lines of the furnishings that would surround them.

Artists have their cycles when they favor various styles. For example, a painter might go through a blue period when he featured that hue. Stickley, too, made adjustments until he modestly seemed to feel that he had climbed to the apex. When a person reaches Utopia, why move anywhere else? His furniture no longer required major revision.

There was one aspect that bothered this man . . . his emulators. Stickley could recite, with disdain, the names of the manufacturers who copied his wares. Watch out for Hand-craft, Mission, Roycroft, Quaint, Arts and Crafts, he warned. It was his opinion that these companies advertised their wares to make the public think they were acquiring the original Craftsman. While Stickley admitted this was a form of flattery, he disliked their aping ways. Worst of all, two competitors shared his family name. They were Leopold and J. George Stickley, his younger brothers. These two were perfectly capable of putting out good products on their own. They advertised that the crafting of furniture was their only business. The skins they acquired for upholstery were so fresh that the goats from which the hides came had recently grazed in fields in Palestine. Their chairs, desks, and tables were not of one standardized size to meet the needs of an average person. They offered customized dimensions to suit customer preference. Perhaps they couldn't accommodate a seven-foot basketball player or a Tom Thumb, but at least there was no Mr. Average in their vocabulary.

Arts and Crafts enthusiasts wanted people to use their hands and be creative instead of relying on machines. While Gustav Stickley disdained professional copycats, he encouraged home hobbies. Women could order his marked fabrics, sold with sufficient floss to create embroidered curtains, dresser scarves, or pillow covers. Men could buy patterns with instructions on how to construct

Craftsman-type furniture. Even the necessary hardware was available to order. Stickley's policy was to discourage copycat competition, but to encourage avocational pursuits.

Stickley Brothers arm rocker made by Quaint Furniture, Grand Rapids, Michigan; 25½" arm to arm, 32" high. In Iowa, **$275.**

Fall-front mission oak desk; 29½" wide, 15½" deep, 60" high. In Iowa, **$695.**

Close-up of brass plate found on mission rocker.

The interior section of a fall-front Stickley Brothers mission desk made by Quaint Furniture of Grand Rapids, Michigan (see brass plate close-up); 34½" wide, 17½" deep, 45" high. In Wisconsin, $595.

One wonders how the name "Mission" came to be the generic name for the furniture that Gustav Stickley carefully developed, when "Craftsman" was the name he registered with the United States government. There are differing versions of the whys and wherefores.

Out in California, across the continent from Stickley's workshop near Syracuse, New York, Spanish monks of long ago worked with their Indian converts to build small missions. Because neither the leaders nor their flock were knowledgeable carpenters, their tables and benches were simply made. Was this the inspiration for the mission style of furniture and the source for the name?

Or was it because of the utilitarian Stickley bungalow with its unfussy and non-fancy style that the title evolved? Some think a promoter who advertised the houses found them plain and called them mission. This moniker clung to the houses and the furniture much as a frightened kindergartner clings to his mother on the first day of school.

There are those who say that each article of furniture has a purpose. It is a chair's function to form a place to sit down. A bed is a place to sleep. Furniture with a reason for being, with a mission, equals mission furniture. At any rate, the Craftsman name did not become the generic (group) title. Mission won.

In 1916, Gustav Stickley was forced to declare bankruptcy. There has been speculation as to why his business did not succeed. His marketing techniques might have harmed him since he sold only through a catalog, "The Craftsman," or at selected stores throughout the country. Maybe he overextended himself by producing too much variety and by constructing a huge new building just before America entered World War I. Perhaps he worked against his own interests when he let amateurs order patterns and supplies instead of selling the completed product to them. No doubt his business suffered when inferior wares made by his competitors sold for less. Also, by the 1920s this type of stark furniture was fading from popularity. Styles and tastes were changing in the postwar world.

Mission oak utility cabinet with spade feet; 20" wide, 15½" deep, 43½" high. In Illinois, $300.

Mission oak stand; 15" square, 28¼" high. In Wisconsin, $135.

Mission-style rocker with label reading, "Quaint Furniture, Stickley Bros. Co., Grand Rapids, Michigan"; 28" arm to arm, 39" high. In Illinois, $395.

Umbrella stand with a mission influence; 10" diameter, 25½" high. In Iowa, $145.

Mission oak hall tree made of quarter-sawed oak with metal hooks and lift-lid storage compartment; 31" wide, 17½" deep, 82" high. In Iowa, $795.

Mission oak fall-front desk; 31¼" wide, 17½" deep, 46½" high. In Iowa, $495.

Golden oak with its fancier lines was around longer than mission. First advertised in 1890, it was still being offered when styles were changing to veneered dark woods in the late 1920s. Mission was first exhibited in 1900, but had nearly exited from the home scene by the 1920s. The golden version experienced a revival of popularity in the 1960s, and mission lagged along behind, not reappearing much until ten years after that.

Gustav Stickley insisted that Craftsman furniture would sell for many times its original price in fifty to one hundred years. His prophecy proved to be true. He believed this because of the fine quality of its construction. He also knew oak forests were being depleted and that fine, solid oak furniture would become hard to get. Some people appreciate his works as examples of an all-American style. A dresser which cost forty-eight dollars new (more west of Denver because of freight charges) may now bring thousands. Please remember, it is Gustav Stickley's work that is especially treasured. Other names—including those of his brothers—have not received that distinction. He was the pacesetter. They copied.

In order to protect his rights, Gustav Stickley registered his mark with the government. In his 1910 "Catalog of Craftsman Furniture Made by Gustav Stickley at the Craftsman Workshops, Eastwood, N.Y.," a somewhat misleading statement appears. This furniture designer emphatically declared, "Furthermore, it should be borne in mind that each piece of Craftsman Furniture is not only tagged with the name 'Craftsman' but is stamped with my registered shop mark—a joiner's compass of ancient make, enclosing the motto 'Als ik Kan,' and bearing my own signature below."

Those who study Craftsman furniture suggest that Stickley's works were not marked with his name in 1900 when the Toby Furniture Company of Chicago marketed his New Art furniture with a circular Toby label.

A short time later a logo was developed and appeared with variations. The Als ik Kan (as I can) motto, surrounded by an an-

Mission oak, rush seated occasional or side chair with exposed pegs. Also available with a leather, slip seat. The trademark Als ik kan *(Dutch motto meaning "As I can") surrounded by an old joiner's compass and Gustav Stickley's signature are stamped in now-faded red on the back upright post. Original price was $7. 36" high. In Illinois,* **$245.**

Mission oak clock; 10½" wide, 4½" deep, 16¼" high. In Iowa, **$185.**

Mission oak clock; 14" wide, 6" deep, 31½" high. In Iowa, **$335.**

cient compass symbol with the maker's last-name signature beneath, appeared as a small red decal in 1902-1903, followed later with "Gustav Stickley" written out. Usually in red, the trademark decal expanded somewhat in size from 1904 to 1912. A burnt-in version, returning to just the name "Stickley" beneath, appeared from 1912 to 1916. The company discontinued its operations in 1916.

Inspect the backs, underneath the arms, and the bottoms of chairs for labels.

Mission-style youth rocker. The name Stickley Brothers, Grand Rapids, Michigan, is burned into the underside of the seat. 31" high. In Illinois, $245.

Mission oak armchair; 25" arm to arm, 36" high. In Illinois, $210.

Mission oak lift-lid necessary chair, also called commode or potty chair; 24½" arm to arm, 35" high. In Illinois, $150.

Mission oak footstool with upholstered top; 18½" wide, 14" deep, 16½" high. In Iowa, $135.

Footstool in the mission oak style; 15¹/₂" wide, 12" deep, 10" high. In Illinois, **$125.**

Pedestal extension table with square, unadorned base; 54" diameter, 29¹/₄" high. In Colorado, **$495.** *Golden oak pressed-back chairs, 39¹/₂" high,* **$145** *each.*

Four-drawer file cabinet with mission-style sides; 18" wide, 24" deep, 52" high. In Iowa, $495.

Smoking stand with mission style; 13" square, 28¼" high. In Illinois, $110.

It is interesting to observe that the leaders mentioned here who had some relationship to the Arts and Craft Movement were artistic, had high ideals, and were almost religious in their outlook. They wanted the furniture in homes to be in harmony with the architectural structure of the dwelling. They opposed cheap, poor quality, machine workmanship. Overornamentation distressed them, and, in general, they promoted hand craftmanship. Indeed, they were men of vision with a mission.

Mission oak smoking stand with slag-type green-and-white glass in door; 17½" wide, 11¼" square top, 28" high. In Illinois, $155.

Glossary

Applied decoration

An ornamentation crafted separately and applied to a piece.

Artificial graining

Paint or stain applied to furniture to imitate the grain of a specific wood.

Atlantes

A supporting pillar designed in the form of a man.

Cabriole leg

A leg with a double curve that bulges at the knee, and flows in and out again at the ankle.

Cane

A long, narrow strip of rattan used for weaving chair seats and backs.

Caryatid

A supporting pillar designed in the form of a woman.

Cheval (chevalle) mirror

A tall mirror supported by an upright frame. A cheval dresser has a mirror of this type set to the side of the hat cabinet.

Chiffonier

A tall, narrow chest of drawers, often called a "highboy" today by collectors.

Chifforobe

An article of furniture made with a chest of drawers on one side and a narrow wardrobe on the other.

Chimera (chimaera)

A fire-breathing creature from Greek mythology with a lion's head, a goat's body, and a serpent's tail. Generally, a horrible creature of the imagination.

Circa (C. or c.)

An approximate date that is used when the exact date is unknown. "Somewhere in the 1920s" could be "circa 1925."

Claw foot

Furniture feet that resemble the claws of a bird.

Closed cupboard

A cupboard with glassless doors. The inside is not visible without opening the doors.

Commode

An enclosed, cupboard type washstand, usually including one or more drawers or doors.

Concave

A surface that curves inwardly.

Convex

A surface that curves outwardly.

Divan

A couch or sofa.

Eclectic

In furniture design the practice of borrowing, combining, or adapting previous styles in order to give latitude to a designer's creativity.

Extension

A table top that pulls apart so leaves may be added to enlarge it.

Fall front

A hinged lid on a desk that drops down to form a writing surface.

Finger hold

A cutout part in the back rail of a chair into which the fingers may be inserted to move the chair.

Finial

A carved, cast, or turned terminal ornament on furniture, clocks, or accessory pieces.

Fretwork

An ornamental border, perforated or cut in low relief.

Gargoyle

A grotesquely carved ornamental creature, projecting from a building, that served as a spout for carrying off rain water. Sometimes, on furniture, grotesques or chimeras are called gargoyles.

Griffin

An imaginary creature with the head, wings, and forelegs of an eagle, and the body, hind legs, and tail of a lion.

Grotesques

Figures or parts of figures of animals and people mixed with flowers, fruits, or foliage created in a fantastic or unnatural way.

Highboy

A tall chest of drawers on legs, often of table height, mounted on another chest of drawers. Usually dates to the eighteenth century.

Hoosier

Now a generic name for a kitchen cabinet with a pullout work surface, meal or flour bins, drawers, sifters, cupboard space, etc. This one-unit cabinet was made in the late 1800s and early 1900s in the Hoosier state, Indiana, and elsewhere.

Incised

A design cut or engraved into the surface.

Marriage

When pieces of furniture are combined as one although not originally intended to be united, such as a bookcase top added to a fall-front desk to form a secretary.

Mullions

Narrow dividing bars between windowpanes or doors of bookcases, china cabinets, and other pieces with glass enclosures.

Ogee

A molding with a continuous double curve.

Paw feet

Furniture feet that resemble the paws of an animal.

Pier mirror

A tall, narrow mirror often hung between two long windows or any other place in the house where one would be able to obtain full image of himself.

Plain sawed

Boards that are cut from the whole log lengthwise in parallel cuts. This results in a pattern of stripes and a series of eliptical V's.

Plank seat

A solid, wooden seat often of one piece of wood.

Pressed back

A design pressed into the back of a chair with a metal die to imitate carving. Pressed designs are also used on other pieces of furniture.

Projection front

A top drawer that protrudes over the rest of the drawers as seen in dressers and washstands.

Quarter sawed

Cutting a log into quarters by splitting it lengthwise and then cutting each half in half again. Then each of these quarters is cut into parallel boards at right angles to the annual growth. Although such cutting wastes wood, the resulting pattern vividly exposes the flakes or pith rays to produce a pronounced pattern.

Rolltop

A flexible panel made of parallel slats that slides up or down in grooves, such as the lid of a desk.

Serpentine

A snakelike curve that is convex at the center and ends and concave between.

Sideboard

A piece of furniture for storing silverware, dishes, linens, or other tableware in a dining area.

Slat

A horizontal crossbar in a chair back.

Splat

The center upright in a chair back.

Splay

Slanting out, as chair legs slant from the seat to the floor.

Stile

The upright piece of a frame or panel in furniture.

Stretcher

The rung or crosspiece that connects cabinet, table, or chair legs.

Swell front

A rounded front in furniture similar to a convex surface.

Taboret (tabourette)

A small plant stand.

Veneer

A thin layer of decorative wood glued over the surface of another wood to add beauty to a piece.

Victorian

Furniture that was made during the reign of England's Queen Victoria (1837-1901). Much was machine made, overly ornamental, and ornate.

Wardrobe

A piece of furniture in which clothes are hung.

Bibliography

Aronson, Joseph. *Encyclopedia of Furniture*. New York, N.Y.: Crown Publishers, Inc., 1965.

Cole, Ann Kilborn. *How To Collect the New Antiques*. New York, N.Y.: David McKay Company, Inc., 1966.

Durant, Mary. *The American Heritage Guide to Antiques*. American Heritage Publishing Co., Inc., 1970.

Grotz, George. *The New Antiques*. Garden City, N.Y.: Doubleday & Company, Inc., 1964.

Israel, Fred L., ed. *1897 Sears, Roebuck Catalogue*. New York, N.Y.: Chelsea House Publishers, 1976.

Mackay, James. *Turn-of-the-Century Antiques*. New York, N.Y.: E. P. Dutton & Co., Inc., 1974.

Miller, Robert W. *Clock Guide Identification with Prices*. Des Moines, Iowa.: Wallace-Homestead Book Co., 1974.

Mirken, Alan, ed. *1927 Sears, Roebuck Catalogue*. New York, N.Y.: Bounty Books div., Crown Publishers, Inc., 1970.

Schroeder, Joseph J., Jr., ed. *Sears, Roebuck & Co. 1908 Catalogue No. 117*. Chicago, Illinois: The Gun Digest Company, 1969.

Stickley Craftsman Furniture Catalogs; Craftsman Furniture Made by Gustav Stickley and *The Work of L. & J. G. Stickley*. Introduction by David M. Cathers. New York, N.Y.: Dover Publications, Inc., 1979.

Material from the Grand Rapids Public Library, Grand Rapids Michigan, included:

Ransom, Frank Edward. *The City Built on Wood, a History of the Furniture Industry in Grand Rapids, Michigan*. Ann Arbor, Michigan: Edwards Bros., Inc., 1955.

And a portion of a leaflet: *"The Story of Grand Rapids, Furniture the Product of Pride."* plus various periodicals from the turn of the century.

Index

About the Authors

When Bob and Harriett Swedberg research and write books, they travel thousands of miles. They meet many fine people who share their interest in preserving heritage articles for future generations. While they enjoy visiting museums, they do not include museum pieces in their books. The Swedbergs photograph only articles that are actually available to the public to purchase or are in the possession of people who have secured them to preserve and collect. To date, this couple has written books on oak, country furniture, wicker, Victorian, and advertising, as well as on refinishing and repairing antiques. They are available as speakers and enjoy teaching about America's heritage through antiques classes.